THE AUTHOR Stephen Walsh was awarded a choral exhibition at Gonville and Caius College, Cambridge University, where he graduated with honors in 1963. He is a free-lance music critic who contributes regularly to *The Listener, The Observer,* and *The Times* of London. He also sings professionally.

THE LIEDER OF SCHUMANN

The Lieder of Schumann

STEPHEN WALSH

PRAEGER PUBLISHERS
New York · Washington

BOOKS THAT MATTER

Published in the United States of America in 1971
by Praeger Publishers, Inc., 111 Fourth Avenue,
New York, N.Y. 10003

© 1971 by Stephen Walsh

All rights reserved

No part of this publication may be reproduced, stored
in a retrieval system or transmitted in any form or by
any means, electronic, mechanical, photocopying, recording
or otherwise, without the prior permission of the Copyright
owner.

Library of Congress Catalog Card Number: 72-154349

Printed in Great Britain

Contents

Introduction		vii
1.	Poet and Pianist	1
2.	Spring	13
3.	The Cycles	32
4.	Autumn	57
5.	Symphonic Interlude	75
6.	Winter	95
7.	The Song-writer	104
Index		125

To My Parents

Introduction

Schumann's reputation, unlike that of many contemporary romantics, is at present enjoying something of a revival. His piano music, it is true, has never really been out of favour. But his other instrumental work, in particular the later chamber music, has for years tottered perilously near to the precipice of complete oblivion. The reawakening of interest in these works, in the symphonies and concertos, and in the big choral–dramatic works of Schumann's closing decade, is tremendously encouraging to those who believe that no balanced assessment of this great composer can possibly be made until we accept both the good and the bad, the familiar and the strange, the spontaneous and the laborious in his music as different facets of the same personality rather than as yardsticks of its well-being at the time of writing.

So far, sad to say, Schumann's songs have not been included in this revival, at any rate in public performance. Singers, who can afford to be conservative in their choice of repertoire, seldom explore beyond well-trodden paths, even in the tempting countryside of Schubert, let alone Schumann. And so we hear performance after performance of the three or four unified cycles which Schumann wrote in 1840, and little or nothing of the admittedly uneven but fascinating and sometimes masterly work of the period 1848–52. It is one object of the present book to give equal coverage to all Schumann's songs, while trying to avoid the special pleading which can so easily, with a composer of his type, devalue positive criticism of the music as a whole. I have tried also to relate the songs as far as possible to Schumann's work in other media, and to suggest how, in my view, they reflect his psychological growth in the dozen or so years spanned by his mature work as a songwriter.

Existing literature on Schumann and his music is plentiful, but I am indebted in particular to three works for information and occasionally ideas; these are Eric Sams's study, *The Songs of Robert Schumann* (Methuen, 1969); Martin Cooper's chapter on the songs in *Schumann, a Symposium* (Oxford U.P., 1952), edited by Gerald Abraham; and Leon B. Plantinga's invaluable *Schumann as Critic* (Yale U.P., 1967). Eric Sams has also written often in *Musical Times*, especially with reference to his theory of ciphers in Schumann's music. His work is also stimulating, sometimes illuminating, often tendentious, but it cannot now be ignored in any serious study of the composer.

Special thanks are due to friends who, consciously or unconsciously, helped me write the book: to Bill and Erika Mann, who were kind and hospitable, as they always are, and their daughter Nicky, who typed some of the MS.; to Alan McNaught, who played through many of the songs with me; and to Richard Sharp of Cassell's, who gave helpful, practical and tolerant advice on matters of presentation and procedure and who bought me slightly more lunches than I bought him. Finally, though they know my face better than my name, I must thank the staff of the Westminster Central Music Library for their unfailing readiness to help with any inquiry, however trivial.

I *Poet and Pianist*

Of the important lieder-composers before Wolf, Schumann has the best reputation for literacy, in the most cultivated sense of that term. He was certainly the best read, though whether his understanding and taste were quite all that tradition suggests is a question to be considered in due course in connection with the songs themselves.

Schumann was literate by circumstantial good fortune. His father ran a book-selling and publishing business in the Saxon town of Zwickau, and also wrote books of his own, including novels, handbooks and translations of the classics, so that Robert was from his earliest youth encouraged not only to read widely but to write and criticize. At the Zwickau Lyceum he belonged to a literary society with the motto 'It is the duty of every man of culture to know the literature of his country'. At home he produced critical essays, plays and poetry, mostly of an imitative nature, but sometimes on a more ambitious scale suggesting that he regarded such things as important and had the tenacity to carry them through. When his father died in 1826, Schumann was still describing his hopes of a creative career in terms of poetry at least as much as music, and his correspondence of this period is literary to a fault, packed with showy allusions and learned references, florid in language and sentiment.

These youthful letters, starting with the ones he wrote to his former schoolfriend Emil Flechsig, who preceded him to Leipzig University in 1827, are the first vital links in the chain of Schumann's mature character. They reveal a young man of acute, even unhealthy sensitivity and a vivid imagination, clever with words yet, by his own admission, unpractised at logical or extended thought. Up to the age of twenty, Schumann wrote in an authentic romantic style, in which triviality of thought and feeling is tricked out by egregious imagery, as if insignificant (and therefore ephemeral) emotion were the one thing above all to be feared. At the same time the one flight from reality leads to another—a love of fantasy and illusion, a verbal impressionism where nothing is tangible or quite what it seems. Both traits seem to have sprung from a direct imitation of Schumann's literary hero of the hour, the novelist Jean Paul Richter. But he never wholly lost his taste for either, and if the second quality was to prove the more personal and fruitful, in both music and music criticism, the first continued to function intermittently in those musical works where the creative flame burnt low.

There are positive and useful characteristics to set against the adolescent extravagance of the Flechsig letters. Schumann was unusual among literary romantics in possessing a lively sense of the absurd, and even his most flamboyant stretches of purple prose lack that crashing solemnity with which so many German (and not only German) writers of the time recorded every last detail of their emotional lives. This is not to say that satire and self-parody figure prominently in his letters, any more than they do in his mature criticisms. But a certain good-humoured objectivity, a deprecatory twinkle in the eye, suggests the ability to stand aside and see himself as others saw him. Later he was to feel a deep need for the approval of others—at once the penalty and the motive of self-analysis. Inward observation was always, however, balanced by outward. Schumann possessed the caricaturist's ability to pick out essentials and use them in quick, telling description. Some of the early letters to his mother, narrating his journeys to Leipzig in 1828 and from there to Heidelberg via a circuitous tour of the Rhine the following year, are fine achievements of descriptive writing, vivid yet economical. And of course his early piano music makes much play with the lightning sketch, the sharp feeling for atmosphere and character which Schumann still attributes (in, for instance, the programme of *Papillons*) to the influence of Jean Paul, but which is indeed uniquely his own.

Schumann's literary inclinations must have led him to think seriously about vocal composition from the start. The one substantial item of juvenilia is a setting of Psalm 150 for soprano, contralto, piano and orchestra, made when he was twelve. But his own instrument was the piano: on this he improvised, sometimes at great length, and at this—at least until 1840—it was his habit to compose. The piano offered peculiar advantages to a young musician caught up in his own moods and fantasies, and Schumann clearly felt able to speak through the notes under his fingers in a way that paralleled his articulateness with the written word. (We have his own testimony of this in a letter of November 1829 to Friedrich Wieck: 'Schubert is ever "my only Schubert", especially as he has so much in common with "my only Jean Paul"; when I play Schubert, I feel as if I were reading one of Jean Paul's novels.' The reference which follows is to a piano work, the four-hand Rondo in A, op. 107.)

Schumann had learnt the piano from the age of seven, when his father had taken him for lessons with the local church organist, Johann Gottfried Kuntzsch. In 1819 father and son travelled to Karlsbad to hear the pianist–composer Ignaz Moscheles, and from this experience seems to date Schumann's ambition to become a virtuoso pianist. Although Kuntzsch found the boy unresponsive to theoretical disciplines, he was a receptive pupil in other respects, and was probably indebted to Kuntzsch for his first introduction to the music of Beethoven, Hummel, Weber, perhaps also Schubert, Haydn and Mozart.

By the time his father died in 1826, Schumann was a skilled and reasonably educated amateur musician, and it was unfortunate for him that his mother took a more conventional view of art as a livelihood, preferring to see him safely launched on a legal career. The four years from 1826 to 1830 were a dangerously upsetting time for a young man so inclined to introspection and nervous depression. Much of the latter part of the period was spent, at Leipzig in 1828 and at Heidelberg the following year, in the wholehearted pursuit of music, while his letters home seek without much conviction to reassure his mother and guardian of his diligence and determination in the study of the law. He also travelled a good deal: not only down the Rhine, but to southern Bavaria, Italy and Switzerland. According to his biographer, Wasielewski, his legal studies consisted of going 'as far as the lecture-room door, pausing and slowly turning away'.

But Schumann's own mind was far from settled. As late as March 1830 he was writing home for permission to stay in Heidelberg an extra six months, before deciding finally on his future. Not until July did he ask his mother to allow him to return to Leipzig for musical study under Wieck. Even his musical direction was uncertain. 'If you knew how my mind is always in a turmoil, and how my symphonies would have reached opus 100, if I had only noted them down,' he wrote to Wieck from Heidelberg in the letter already quoted; and 'sometimes I am so full of music that I find it simply impossible to write anything down'. Elsewhere his letters leave no doubt that he regarded himself as a pianist, and the decisive one to his mother the following July is still guarded about his creative gifts, though it was in his interests to convey a mood of confidence and certainty about his future in music. The truth is that he was paying for his earlier lack of discipline. Even by 1827 the urge to create his own music as an extension of re-creating other people's was making itself felt, but he could not collect or control his thoughts sufficiently for a steady flow of finished compositions to result. It was only in the early summer of 1830 that music began to appear in quantity on paper, culminating in the eventual op. 1, the '*Abegg*' *Variations* for solo piano, and this would seem to mark the point of no return. Significantly, the works of this period form a more definite pattern than anything written earlier, a pattern dominated by the piano. It was to be maintained until Schumann next turned to the voice no less than ten years later.

But although the few compositions completed before 1830 may hardly be what Schumann would later have cared to regard as typical products of a teenage romantic genius, they are of interest to us because they include some songs. The earliest of these, composed in 1827, were inspired by the singing of one of Robert's musical friends, Frau Agnes Carus, who was at that time living in Colditz but moved to Leipzig the following year on her husband's appointment as Professor of Medicine at the university. Further songs written in 1828 are mostly settings of poems by Justinus Kerner, though we have Schumann's assurance that they were inspired by a group of Jean Paul settings by Gottlob Wiedebein, to whom he sent them for comment in July 1828. (Curiously, Schumann himself never set any Jean Paul; possibly he felt unequal to the task, or perhaps he considered that only the piano could properly express his feelings for this 'child of dissolute Dionysus and delicate Camoene'.) Wiedebein took an encouraging view of the songs, swayed no doubt by an implication in Schumann's letter that he was completely untrained in music.* To the modern student, however, hoping for a glimpse of Schumann's later genius as a song-writer or at least some flash of the elusive inspiration of the early piano works, they are a disappointment, showing that—far from being inspired by words—he was at this stage still hopelessly fettered by the need to contain his keyboard improvisor's fantasy. Now and then the piano comes forward with a phrase which seems to crystallize a real and individual statement about the poem. But for the most part the accompaniments know their place: a few chords, repeated or plain, chromatic harmonies, heavily dependent on the diminished seventh chord, and in one case a sextuplet arpeggio figure which looks, but does not sound, like Schubert—these are all the evidence of the young Schumann's fertile keyboard imagination. The short postludes, by the future composer of *Dichterliebe*, are in most cases inept, and in one case ('Sehnsucht') missing presumed unwritten.

The voice parts, on the other hand, possess a certain jejune charm, especially in those songs which Schumann composed through, following the changing pattern of the verses. In these one senses him responding to the words, in detail as well as spirit, whereas in the strophic songs the tunes often give the impression of having been independently conceived. 'Sehnsucht', which bears the earliest date (June 1827), is in simple strophic form with a quite unrelated piano introduction:

* The songs submitted were probably 'Kurzes Erwachen', 'Gesanges Erwachen', and one of two entitled 'An Anna' ('Lange harrt' ich'). Schumann may also have enclosed some or all of his earlier efforts. The present discussion is based on the six songs published by Universal Edition under the editorship of Karl Geiringer in 1933 (which include the Kerner settings listed above), and the three which Brahms included in the supplementary volume of the Collected Edition published in 1893. These songs, together with two others composed in 1829, were graced by Schumann with the Roman opus number II.

Later Schumann shows himself interested in varying this scheme, either making an altered setting of the last verse or preferring a ternary form, or even in one case writing a lengthy song in free-form, not unlike a concert aria. This last is the 'An Anna' sent to Wiedebein, who might have been forgiven for dismissing it as formless or chaotic, but instead managed the encouraging admonishment, 'Wild plants may grow wild; nobler fruits need care.' Schumann's versatile use of strophic, ternary and unitary forms became a feature of his mature song-writing.

He was later able to make practical use of three of these early songs in piano works of the early 1830s. The second 'An Anna' in F major supplied, with changes only of detail and key, the second movement of the piano sonata in F sharp minor, op. 11, while 'Im Herbste', more fully recomposed, became the Andantino of the G minor sonata, op. 22. 'Hirtenknabe', with its quaint little folk-tune, became no. 4 of the six intermezzi, op. 4. In each case the music seems happier with the voice part transferred to the piano, partly, no doubt, because of the composer's increased maturity and skill in making the changes. In several of the 1840 songs, as we shall see, the voice part is actually redundant as far as musical completeness is concerned, but it can seldom be argued that the music would be improved by leaving the voice out, and this marks a decisive difference between the vocal piano music of Schumann's apprentice and mature periods.

The early burst of song-writing soon fell away after the Wiedebein correspondence, and from 1830 for a decade Schumann completed only works for solo piano, his first twenty-three opus numbers being for that instrument. The reasons for this extraordinary singlemindedness are important, because they also throw light on the scarcely less remarkable conversion to song in 1840, to symphony in 1841, to chamber music in 1842, and even to opera and cantata later on. So far as we can judge, circumstance and psychology played a roughly equal part, as so often with Schumann. The first thing to note about the piano music of 1830-40 is not its quality, which though often high is variable, nor even its originality, which is by any standards great, but the unique impression it gives of being a diary of its composer's mental and physical life. We know from his letters, especially those to his future wife, Clara Wieck, that he used music in this way. But even if such evidence were lacking, the music itself, with its sketchbook swiftness and economy, its conversational blend of small talk and deep feeling, its concern to record rather than discuss, and its extreme intimacy of expression, might prompt the same conclusion. 'It is very strange,' he wrote to Clara in April 1828, 'but if I write much to you, as I am doing now, I cannot compose. The music all goes to you.' And a few days earlier: 'Everything that goes on in the world affects me, politics, literature, people; I think it all over in my own way, and anything that can be turned into music finds expression in that way.' He would even interpret other composers in this light. To Wieck he wrote, in that revealing letter of November 1829 already quoted twice: 'What a diary is to others for jotting down all their passing emotions, his music-paper was to Schubert.' And Schumann was thinking especially of Schubert's piano music, not his songs, about which he had reservations.

The journalistic quality of Schumann's piano works recalls that in his student days, and before, most of his composition was done extempore at the keyboard, with little recourse to music-paper. One imagines him leaping to the piano to release passing emotions of anger, affection or humour in precisely the circumstances that, with a non-creative person of the twentieth century, might provoke a memorandum or a telephone-call.

But if the piano appealed by virtue of its convenience, flexibility and eloquence in the recording of musical common-places, it had the additional merit of familiarity. For all his youthful adventurousness of spirit, Schumann suffered deep-rooted insecurities of personality, which increased with age. He was, as we have seen, self-aware to a morbid degree, and needed the approval of others for his work and for his actions. Yet he could also be exaggeratedly self-effacing. After Mendelssohn's appointment as conductor of the Leipzig Gewandhaus concerts in 1835, Schumann allowed himself to be dazzled by the genius and flair of the young Berliner, and his letters show regret that he lacked Mendelssohn's advantages of background and upbringing, rather than conviction that he could nevertheless achieve comparable things. Similarly, after his marriage (though not apparently before) he sometimes found Clara's brilliance and fame as a pianist a check on his own creative work, the urge to compose being on such occasions replaced by a brooding unease which, after a tour of Russia in 1844, induced a severe nervous collapse. As he grew older Schumann became increasingly reserved and silent in company, and for most of his life he was an inadequate conductor and rehearser largely because he could not express himself articulately or personably, if at all. There is evidence, too, that his teaching suffered for the same reason.

Insecurity bred caution and conservatism, traits which became as typical of Schumann in his personal work and behaviour as they were untypical of him in his progressive role as co-founder of the *Neue Zeitschrift für Musik*, a paper committed to young art, the future and the fight against philistinism.* This paradox is akin to the contrast between Schumann's quiet social manner and his very positive, even idiosyncratic, keyboard style, and it may be significant that the two creative outlets of the thirties—piano improvisation (or improvisatory composition) and written criticism—both began to lose their value to him at about the same time, though for practical reasons he could not relinquish his responsibilities towards the *Zeitschrift* until 1844. Their main feature in common was perhaps that they were youthful enterprises; the piano represented the waywardness or dream-fantasy of youth, the paper its idealism. In the late 1830s Schumann aged, or at least mellowed, quite rapidly, and marriage came at a time when he was psychologically ready for domesticity: the metaphorical slippers and pipe replacing the all too real champagne and

---

* The *NZfM* began publication on 3 April 1834 with Julius Knorr as its first editor. Schumann took over as editor at the start of 1835 and held the post until his retirement nine and a half years later.

cigars of his student days. The year of their marriage, 1840, was as it happens also the year of Clara's twenty-first birthday, and she too had by then outgrown musical charades and secret messages.

Some new medium of expression was always, therefore, in the wind after their secret engagement in August 1837, just before Clara became eighteen. At first Schumann had the idea of turning to chamber music, and in 1838–9 he began no fewer than four string quartets, all now lost. 'I am myself looking forward to the quartets,' he wrote to Clara in March 1838. 'The piano is getting too limited for me.' In the same letter he noted also an increasing interest in melody. We can trace the tendency in works completed about this time: the C major *Fantasie* (1836–8); some of the *Fantasiestücke*, op. 12 (1837); *Kreisleriana* (1838), where the capricious and often fragmentary themes of *Carnaval* and *Davidsbündlertänze* are replaced by broad, structural melody which binds the figuration in quite a new way. Again, it is significant that the *Fantasie* and *Fantasiestücke* were conceived during times of real unhappiness for Schumann, of separation from Clara and yearning for her, while the *Davidsbündlertänze* date from just after the reconciliation and secret pledge, and *Kreisleriana* from a few months later still (April 1838), when he was beginning once again to feel her absence on tour.

In *Kreisleriana*, melody grows in an organic way out of the very heart of Schumann's piano style—perhaps the earliest foreshadowing of song as a main current in his work. Yet it was almost a further two years (so far as is known for certain) before he composed the first songs, and when they came it was precisely as though a barrier had been removed. The barrier, of course, was in Schumann's mind. The piano had served him for so long and so intimately that he simply could not bring himself to confide in any other medium, until the need was too pressing to resist. His much-quoted letters of the period seem to confirm this. The famous one of June 1839 to Hermann Hirschbach, in which he places vocal music well below instrumental music in the artistic hierarchy, while advising Hirschbach to write more for the voice, shows that for him the barrier was still up in the year before his marriage. The 1840 letters tell quite a different story. 'Ah, Clara,' he wrote in

February, in the first flush of *Myrten*, 'what bliss it is writing for the voice; and I have had to do without it for so long!' And to Gustav Keferstein that same month: 'I can hardly tell you what a joy it is to write for the voice compared with instrumental composition.'

Many reasons have been advanced, some plausible, others less so, for the suddenness of this conversion. Among the former type is Eric Sams's ingenious suggestion that a meeting with Mendelssohn on 31 January 1840 prompted a discussion of Schumann's views on song-writing and drove him to his newly acquired copy of Schlegel's Shakespeare for an experimental setting of Feste's closing song from *Twelfth Night* ('Schlusslied des Narren', op. 127, no. 5, dated 1 February 1840).* More facile is the view that Schumann wrote songs in his bliss at marrying Clara. Apart from its elastic chronology (the marriage took place in September 1840; the early months of that year were months of tension and frequent separation), the argument fails to explain the equation between happiness and song. The evidence of the piano music points indeed to an opposite conclusion. Or if Schumann's anxious and suppressed love is thought sufficient explanation, it must be shown why the change took place in February 1840, instead of at any time in the previous two years. Yet another idea, that Schumann's imagination had declined to such an extent as to necessitate the use of texts as an aid to musical thought, is invalidated by the quality both of the recent pre-1840 piano works and of the songs of that year. *Dichterliebe*, whatever else it may be, is certainly not the work of a creative gift in decline. Admittedly Schumann had an expressive problem. If he felt the piano to be no longer equal to his needs, behind this doubt lurked the fear that people could not understand his music, that it was too obscure and would make no headway. His letters to Clara are full of admonitions to play the more popular works oftener, and in June 1840 he wrote to W. H. Rieffel: 'I was delighted with your remarks about my piano work. If only I could find more people who understood my meaning! I hope that in this I shall do better with songs.' He had previously scorned verbal explanations of music, preferring to allow the listener's imagi-

---

* 'Schumann's Year of Song', *Musical Times*, February 1965.

nation to take its own course. Vocal music meant directness and explicit tone-painting—the power of words, so well known to Schumann, and, we might add, the power of conciseness. He himself had observed that it was his individual character-pieces—the *Fantasiestücke*, for instance—which were best received by musicians at large.

This was in many ways distressing to him, since his own ambitions had always lain in the direction of extended instrumental composition, for which he was now beginning to learn that he had only a moderate talent. His remarks to Hirschbach about song-writing recall that in the *Zeitschrift* he seldom reviewed songs, though significantly he began to do so more often from about 1840. It may be true, as Leon B. Plantinga has suggested,* that Schumann changed direction because he suddenly realized that instrumental music had no future, a view which is at least borne out by his concurrent interest in other vocal forms, the part-song, choral music and opera, also more indirectly by his fondness for making large vocal works out of collections of short ones, much as he had already done at the piano. But such rational motives hardly accord with what we know of Schumann's normal approach to composition, which was typically romantic in its obedience to passing sensations and emotions and much less governed by theory than his prose writings might have us believe. It has to be remembered that if in 1840 he believed suddenly and only in vocal music, he changed his mind again no less abruptly the following year, when symphonic music became his exclusive concern. Song then fell out of favour for another eight years.

Perhaps in the end no tidy explanation need be sought. Most of us have at one time or another felt an urge towards change being inhibited by intuitive affection for the status quo, or by idleness or uncertainty. Intentions may linger for years, frequently denied, until a sudden burst of enthusiasm or energy, a change in circumstance or attitude, brings them to fruition. Schumann's tendency towards a more explicit melodic style than that of his earlier piano works is documented not only in his correspondence of the period but also, as we have seen, in the music itself from 1836. But it was not in his nature

---

* *Schumann as Critic* (Yale U.P., 1967).

to abandon the creative habits of a decade until the need was too strong to resist. Whether or not the final impetus came from outside, the need was always and essentially an internal matter, and it was almost certainly Schumann's innate conservatism, his fear of the unfamiliar and his automatic association of creative work with the one instrument he was himself able to play which prevented him from crossing the Rubicon earlier.

2   *Spring*

The exact number of songs composed by Schumann in 1840 is still uncertain, since many of those written in that year were withheld from publication until later in his life or after his death. It is known, however, that by the end of December at least 126 songs had been completed, and by 31 January 1841—a year after the earliest dated manuscript—the certain minimum is 133. Although Wolf also wrote his songs in brief, explosive bursts, the only greater yield in a single twelvemonth is Schubert's 144 in 1815. But Schubert went on composing songs (another 100 or so in 1816, with his greatest still ahead of him). Schumann stopped almost dead in 1841, and his first year's output includes not only more than half the final total but also most of the finest specimens.

If this seems remarkable to us it was no less so to him. 'I have again composed so much,' he wrote to Clara on 15 May, 'that it seems quite uncanny at times.' 'Sometimes,' he added a fortnight later, 'I feel as if I were coming upon quite new ways in music.' At the end of May he was at work on *Dichterliebe*, having just completed the Eichendorff *Liederkreis*, two works where inspiration is clearly white hot. The fifty or so songs written before May, while equally reflecting the bewildered excitement of the contemporary letters, do so more haphazardly, as if the composer's technical means have not yet caught up with the unexpected surge of creative activity. The main products of these early weeks are the Heine *Liederkreis*, completed before the end of February and already published in May as op. 24 (Schumann's first opus for anything but piano), and *Myrten*, op. 25, which is less a cycle than an anthology, and which Schumann had printed by September as a wedding-present for Clara. These two somewhat uneven collections, together with a handful of other songs some of which could well have found their way into *Myrten*, represent Schumann's first phase of song-writing—a period of experiment and the flexing of long-disused muscles, but also a period of some wonderful songs, including many unfairly neglected by modern singers.

From the start Schumann showed himself conscious of his literary responsibilities. Instead of opening his account with a representative cross-section of contemporary German lyric poems, he plunged in with Shakespeare, Goethe, translations of Burns and Byron, and Heine, the most pungent and perhaps the most influential literary figure of the day. Of these poets only Shakespeare can have aroused his wholehearted personal sympathy, and that partly because of his remoteness in time and his universality of feeling. Goethe was too cool, too spiritual, Burns too stark, Byron too grand, Heine too sceptical for the kindly, sentimental, domestic Schumann of early 1840. Yet the only Shakespeare setting is a slight one of Feste's song, a conceit rather than a personal utterance; while of the others only Goethe failed to draw songs of lasting importance from Schumann's pen.

The Shakespeare song, 'Schlusslied des Narren' ('When that I was and a little tiny boy'), is scarcely more than a trial run, and Schumann kept it back from publication until 1854, when it came out as one of the *Lieder und Gesänge*, op. 127. No doubt he chose the poem as one intended to be sung rather than spoken, perhaps also because it calls for strophic setting (i.e., with the same tune to each verse). But although the result has no special artistic value, technically it is of some interest. The piece is a tiny scherzo in three verses with a tune which, though written like so many lieder in imitation of folk-song, is ultimately rather urbane. For one thing, each verse ends differently, not because the words call for changes of inflexion but apparently because the composer cannot resign himself to the absolute plainness of true folk-music; for another, the song is full of such studied effects as the manufacturing of the voice's third phrase by repeating its first a semitone higher. Furthermore the tune lacks the rhythmic squareness of a folk-song, the composer having ensured this by drawing out the last line of each verse and introducing his piano postlude half a bar earlier than the ear expects. Schumann's clown is something of a pixie. The piano's grace-notes and dotted dance rhythms give him pointed ears and a hopping gait (perhaps suggested by Schlegel's rendering of 'with a hey, ho' as 'hop heisa, hop heisa'). But the accompaniment as a whole is dull, as if Schumann were consciously repressing his natural style. The voice is doubled, or accompanied by simple chords, throughout.

The selection of twenty-six songs in *Myrten* is apparently random, though once his choice was made Schumann arranged them in key sequence with a dedication at the start ('Widmung') and an envoi at the end ('Zum Schluss'), both in A flat. Perhaps the most striking thing about the collection is its diversity of subject. Apart from the Eichendorff *Liederkreis*, the most naturalistic and metaphorical of the song-collections, Schumann's other 1840 cycles are entirely about love: the pain of separation, the agony of non-requital, the ecstasy of marriage. In *Myrten* there are songs about all these aspects of feeling: songs of deprivation, bridal songs, love-songs translated into intense images of nature, and more light-hearted love-songs—all reflecting some part of Schumann's own struggle for Clara's hand. But other feelings and activities are described as well: the more down-to-earth promptings which drive a man to drink, or sport, or battle, the mysterious affections of romantic melancholy and hymnic exaltation. There is even a musical parlour-game. Clearly, as he handed Clara the finely bound volume on the glorious September morning of his wedding, Schumann was in every sense giving himself in all his moods, real and assumed. It was a gift she knew well how to treasure.

Perhaps ten of these songs rank with the noblest Schumann ever wrote, but sadly the five Goethe settings from the *West-östlicher Divan* are not among them. Partly this can be explained by the earliness of the songs and the apparently conscious triviality of the choice of poems, as if the composer were still experimenting and anxious to avoid too intimate an engagement of his feelings. But Schumann never got on well with Goethe in his heart of hearts. He later expended many working hours and much sweated labour on a musical version of *Faust* which captures none of the play's dramatic force and little of its vision, and the 1849 *Wilhelm Meister* songs, though full of memorable invention, are very uneven in quality. Once only, in the 'Nachtlied', op. 96, no. 1, Schumann's last Goethe setting, does he achieve anything like a Schubertian purity of vision akin to that of the verse, and comparison with his other songs of 1850 suggests that it was at some cost to his own natural expression.

Of the *Divan* songs, only 'Talismane' attempts a visionary distillation, and the result is rhetorical rather than sublime. The music recalls that Schumann was an admirer of Mendelssohn's oratorios. But as in Feste's song the listener is made too conscious of the creative mechanism: the resonant triadic melody proclaiming God's omnipotence, the grandiose piano chords, the meandering quavers to describe the poet's confused wandering, the repeated Amens, the neat rondo form—all flawless in their way, yet unmistakably contrived. Altogether preferable, because unselfconscious, is the jaunty 'Freisinn', an open-air song of a type common among Schumann's lieder. 'Freisinn' is really a piano piece, which is perhaps why the composer sounds more at his ease. The voice copies each of the first two piano phrases, and it is the 'accompaniment', with its tiny interludes, which saves the song from squareness. Incidentally, the ternary ABA form is achieved, as so often in Schumann, by ending with a repeat of the poet's first verse.

The same device occurs in two of the remaining *Divan* songs, the tiny drinking-song, 'Sitz' ich allein', and the more lengthy 'Lied der Suleika', whose form is a rondo-like ABABA with the final reprise accommodated by a verse repeat.* Both these songs, like 'Freisinn', seem to have been written at the piano (though Schumann told Clara that he had started composing away from the keyboard), and in the Suleika song only insignificant notes in the voice part are not doubled by the accompaniment. Here, too, we find what is probably one of the first examples in Schumann of a true postlude composed in that intimate, communing style which he later perfected in *Dichterliebe*. To modern ears, this particular song is perhaps too opulently cloaked in its flowing A major robes, for all the shapeliness of the melody. The harmonies match the comfortable sentiments of the poem, but Schumann must have realized that he was courting a certain smugness of effect, for he tried to raise the emotional temperature by accelerating into the climax of each B section. Again the result has an affectation which suits only too well the sentiments expressed.

---

* The poem, 'Wie mit innigstem Behagen', is now usually attributed to Marianne von Willemer, the real-life Suleika of the *Divan*.

The drinking-song is the first of a pair, tiny and epigrammatic in Schumann's best *Carnaval* vein and with not a note out of place. In 'Sitz' ich allein', unlike 'Freisinn', it is the piano whose music is squarely phrased and the voice which lends variety, and a certain bibulous charm, by entering at unexpected moments. The hiccoughing introduction figure delightfully sets the whole scene in five notes. The companion piece, 'Setze mir nicht', is one of the most original songs in *Myrten* and also one of Schumann's wittiest. In its twenty-seven bars it limns to perfection the changing mask of drunkenness—its coarse aggression, its insinuating friendliness, its belching hilarity—and in so doing creates a novel and authentic song-form out of the two verses of the poem. Both these songs deserve more frequent performance.

From Goethe Schumann turned to Robert Burns, a German edition of whose poems had just appeared in Leipzig, translated by Wilhelm Gerhard. Apart from the strange idea of a German composer's setting Burns to music, there are a number of significant features of this choice. Burns's poems are starkly tragic, economical, atmospheric, yet a wonderful synthesis of folk simplicity and high art—sentiment unseduced by sentimentality—and again Schumann's literary training stood him in good stead, enabling him to penetrate the inevitably rather featureless translations and capture the essence of the original verse. Burns also has suggestive musical qualities. His poetry lilts and swings with irresistible rhythm, and it is no accident that Englishmen tend to know poems like 'O, my luve's like a red, red rose' chiefly by their associated melodies.

Schumann's nine Burns songs, all but one of which (his own setting, 'Dem roten Röslein', of the poem just mentioned) are in *Myrten*, owe much to the intrinsic musical qualities of the verse, especially its decisive rhythm and primary emotional colouring. We can see this, above all, in the fact that no less than four of them are strophic—at a time when Schumann was consciously investigating more subtle song-forms. His strophic form is sometimes even simpler than Burns's. 'Hochländers Abschied' ('Farewell to the Highlands'), for instance, has four verses to a fine swinging tune in a bold, tonic–dominant B minor, changing to the major for the third verse's mellowed farewell to the mountains, where a true setting of Burns would require two such tunes, one for each verse and one for the chorus (which Schumann repeats only once, at the end). 'Niemand' ('I hae a Wife o' my Ain') on the other hand has a long tune which fits two verses of the poem. There is also a rather special harmonic flavour about the songs which may suggest some remote folk-memory of bagpipes and highland reels. 'Hochländisches Wiegenlied' ('The Highland Balou') has a drone bass—though on dominant rather than tonic—and soft dissonant harmonies which are decidedly picturesque by early-nineteenth-century standards:

Both 'Hauptmanns Weib' ('The Captain's Lady') and 'Die Hochländer-Witwe' ('The Highland Widow's Lament') start with an arresting E minor triad, in the manner of a call to arms, an effect which stayed in Schumann's mind long enough for him to use it again in several other songs of this year, most notably 'Der arme Peter' and 'Nun hast du mir den ersten Schmerz getan' in *Frauenliebe und -leben*.

But it is not for their special effects that the Burns songs are, as a group, so memorable. Their most distinctive quality, as with the poems themselves, is their emotional truth. Schumann was always artist enough to make good music out of an elegant but affected lyric such as 'Lied der Suleika', but in such circumstances he could also be dangerously perceptive, writing music which acts like an aerial photograph in uncovering the surface lie. In Burns there are no such untruths to reveal, though his poetry is certainly not without its ironies, as for instance in 'The Highland Balou', where in a gentle lullaby the mother insinuates murderous propaganda into her child's subconscious. Schumann quite rightly made no attempt to mirror this contrast in his music, whose smooth rocking reflects the form rather than the content of the poem, and in so doing stresses the irony. Singers should note that both here and elsewhere Burns's own dialect English can without too much difficulty be fitted to the music.

On the debit side is a certain impersonality of feeling, as though the composer were sensitively, often beautifully, reacting to another's emotions rather than engaging his own. This is almost invariably true where harmony or melody now strike us as archaic or in some other way remote, as in the breathless 'Die Hochländer-Witwe', which lucidly portrays the widow's distracted grief but just fails to arouse sympathy for it; or even in the enchanting 'Dem roten Röslein', which languishes with 'Jasminenstrauch' in the otherwise mediocre op. 27. It is much less true in two songs which struck an obvious chord in Schumann's own experience: 'Jemand' ('For the sake o' somebody'), and 'Weit, weit' ('The bonie lad that's far awa' '), both laments of a girl separated from her lover. 'Jemand', which Schumann may have seen in some (essentially facetious) relationship with 'Niemand', is a highly original song in declamatory style, and a rare example in 1840 Schumann of true vocal writing, with the piano part subordinate. Words and music go in perfect accord: the melancholy opening phrase rising to a significant stress on 'Jemand' (cf. the similar accents on 'Niemand' in the companion song), then the same music repeated a fourth higher as though in mounting protest, followed by a new theme in triplets, a lament in the relative major (G) and an outburst of defiance in E minor. Out of this treatment a novel form emerges. The first theme is reprised in the tonic major (hope: the positive aspect of sorrow—compare Burns's 'Ye powers that smile on virtuous love'); then the music jumps straight to the defiant theme now in the dominant—a pun which is both verbal and musical; and at the close Schumann finds the perfect idea—rising in pitch, dynamic and rhythmic tension—to convey the poet's ecstatic avowal of love and devotion.

The strophic 'Weit, weit' is comparatively simple and folkish, but for all that touching. The composer must have imagined some distantly heard song of the hills, for the vocal *tessitura* is high and yearning, the piano's right-hand octaves suggest a romantic orchestral accompaniment and the postlude introduces the scotch-snap, on a richly textured subdominant-sixth chord which portrays with disturbing intensity the coldness and loneliness of separation. Beside this the rather bland 'Im Westen', again about parted lovers, is disappointing. Its music was conceived for the piano, and in its second half—even though there is no solo writing for it—the piano has such musical interest as there is.

Soon after making his first Goethe settings and within at most a week of turning to song, Schumann had his first musical encounter with Heine, the poet who more than any other was to prove his good genius during 1840. Of solo songs composed during this year, no fewer than thirty-seven are to poems by Heine. As with Burns, the conjunction has its unexpected side. Heine was one of the best German lyric poets of his day, and Schumann was evidently excited by the compelling beauty and precision of his imagery. But Heine also imported into lyric verse a unique sense of bitter irony, coupled with an ambiguity of feeling—the lovesickness aroused by Francis Thompson's Daisy, who:

> Left me marvelling why my soul
>   Was sad that she was glad;
> At all the sadness in the sweet,
>   The sweetness in the sad.

In German poetry one form of this device is known as *Stimmungsbrechung* ('mood-breaking'), which lurks in the final line of an innocent lyric like the sting in an insect's tail. A familiar example is 'Wenn ich in deine Augen seh' ', which Schumann set in *Dichterliebe*: when I look into your eyes, sings Heine, all my sorrow vanishes; but when you say 'I love you'

I cannot help weeping bitterly. Schumann's love-life, like Heine's, had had its ups and downs, the latter especially during 1836 and 1837, when Clara sent back all his letters with a request for her own in return, and Robert took up with the Scottish pianist Robena Laidlaw in a decidedly Heinesque spirit of revenge. But his character, with all its complexities and insecurities, was without cynicism, perhaps because it lacked a true perception of the quality of evil. He was capable of dislike, even hatred, when he felt himself personally or his ideals threatened, but there is little evidence of irrational animosity—the purely chemical interaction of sympathy and antipathy. His failure to comprehend fundamental evil was, as we shall see in his ballads, one reason for his inability to compose good dramatic music. The Heine settings often miss, therefore, the pungency of the original verse, while revelling in its vivid and sensitive expressions of feeling, its aptness of imagery, and in particular its avoidance of the Scylla and Charybdis of contemporary German poetry, sententiousness and bathos.

Heine was a considerable narrative poet as well as a lyricist of genius, but Schumann—a miniaturist in spite of himself— was always at his best in brief, and the Heine songs are no exception. The ballads and romances, of which there are five, are of very unequal quality. 'Belsatzar', which may have been Schumann's first Heine setting (though only published six years later, as op. 57), is also the longest, not counting the composite 'Tragödie' and 'Der arme Peter', and it displays, alongside some memorable music, almost every fault that stood between Schumann and satisfactory vocal composition on a large scale. The voice part is thoroughly four-square, and although it makes a reasonably grateful and characteristic line to sing, it leaves little impression on the memory. The piano music on the other hand is consistently exciting and atmospheric until required to characterize actual evil behaviour—the orgiastic drinking of the vassals, Belshazzar's blasphemy or, at the end, his murder—when it lapses impotently into block chords and conventional rhetoric.

The two Heine ballads in op. 49, 'Die beiden Grenadiere' and 'Die feindlichen Brüder', were composed only two or three months later, in May and April respectively, and they too are flawed works of some musical power. In both cases, however, extra conciseness brings some reward. The strange tale of the feuding brothers is set in simple ABAA form, with square, hammered rhythms and an elemental harmonic palette for the fight itself, and more ingratiating music for the Gräfin Laura, who we gather is the cause of the quarrel. The result may not be subtle, but it has a certain grim ferocity. Much more piquant is the grenadiers' song, justly the best-known of Schumann's ballads. In his youth Heine had been a profound admirer of Napoleon, and his poem about the two French soldiers who learn of Napoleon's capture on their way back from Moscow has for once no intended irony. But Schumann is more ambiguous. The music portrays a dead march, solemn and respectful, the rhythm vividly suggestive of disciplined grief. But in melody and harmony the sliding chromatics have just the faintest hint of parody, and after the famous quotation of the 'Marseillaise' near the end the brief piano postlude, with its acid harmonies, can also sound sarcastic:

We may imagine what Schumann thought of a soldier who could express indifference to the fate of his wife and child.

The remaining Heine ballad of this period is 'Der arme Peter', which really falls into a category somewhere between the ballad and the narrative cycle. The three short songs frame an implied story of a young man who goes to see his beloved married to another man and afterwards wanders off to commit suicide—a recurrent situation in both Heine and Schumann (cf. especially 'Das ist ein Flöten und Geigen'). Here *Stimmungsbrechung* and irony both play their part, but for some reason Schumann is dead to everything but the irony of the first poem, where Hans and Grete dance to a brilliant hurdy-gurdy waltz oblivious of their heartbroken onlooker (the first two piano chords are an obvious reference to Schubert's 'Der

Leiermann'). The apparently callous postlude is exactly right for the poem. The other two songs, however, are a sorry anticlimax. No. 2 is of interest for its gradual deceleration from start to finish, the opposite of a device common in Schumann's songs. But neither here nor in the last song, with its relentless doubling of voice and piano, does the invention rise above the mediocre. The slow *accelerando* is a feature of 'Belsatzar' and also of 'Abends am Strand', which was probably composed at about the same time as 'Der arme Peter'. In this unusual romance, Schumann imagined Heine's story-teller gradually increasing his hold on the listener's attention with his quaint (not to say provincial) tales of foreign parts. Wasielewski took Schumann sternly to task for setting such a poem. But there is a great deal of less interesting music in his songs, and the end, with its sudden return to the winding, Bach-like theme and tempo of the opening, vividly conveys the idea of oncoming darkness and the story-teller breaking off to go indoors.

Schumann's best Heine songs are, of course, the short lyrics, of which he composed a round dozen in this first phase, three of them included in *Myrten* while the rest make up the *Liederkreis*, op. 24. The earliest of the *Myrten* settings is probably 'Was will die einsame Träne', but this delicately chromatic song, though characteristic of Schumann in his *soirée* mood, is not at all typical of the Heine settings, and pales into insignificance beside its companions, 'Die Lotosblume' and 'Du bist wie eine Blume'. These short songs are certainly among the finest in all Schumann, and they have much in common. Both adopt the poet's flower-image as a metaphor for the beloved Clara, and in both the almost sacramental atmosphere of awe and devotion leads to a harmonic texture at once richer and plainer than in almost any previous work by Schumann. The idea of a heartbeat is also central to both songs. In later Schumann, repeated chords often betoken a failure of invention on the composer's part. But here the image is exact. In 'Die Lotosblume' the richly textured right-hand chords gradually build up emotional tension until the climactic moment when the moon, the flower's lover, appears and the music modulates thrillingly from the subdominant of F to the subdominant of A flat—perhaps the most effective use Schumann ever made of a device culled from Schubert. 'Du bist wie eine Blume' is in a sense more innocent, less sensual, in its appeal. Technically it is superior to its companion in that no word of the text is repeated, the somewhat lame reiteration of the final line of 'Die Lotosblume' ('for love and the sorrow of love'—an antithesis for which, incidentally, the music has no equivalent) being replaced by a short, rather more chromatic postlude for the piano.

Perhaps no songs in Schumann's oeuvre give clearer indication of his sharp response to poetry which held a special meaning for him, composed as they were within days of the coolly impressive Burns songs and the relatively slight Goethe ones. Even the *Liederkreis* contains nothing so charged, nor anything remotely similar, though the poet is the same. This is much more of a cycle, designed for integral performance, than *Myrten*, being arranged not only in key sequence but with some uniformity of subject, if without any suggestion of narrative or a single situation as in Schubert's cycles or Beethoven's *An die ferne Geliebte*, always a source work for Schumann. The linking idea is love, but especially the pain of separation—a favourite theme of romantic poets, who liked to contemplate the stars or gaze down the river and feel that nature was working to bring lovers together. Schumann had sympathy with such a theme, though by February 1840 it had lost the worst of its poignancy for him, and this may explain why some of the selected poems quickened his creative sense while in others the response is cool. It may also explain the oddity of the choice itself. Aphorisms such as 'Morgens steh' ich auf' and 'Lieb' Liebchen' consort oddly with the extravagant and virtually unsettable 'Warte, wilder Schiffsmann', and the music for these songs confirms that no uniform impulse lay behind their selection, as it clearly did with the Eichendorff *Liederkreis*. Taking a broad view, we can argue that op. 24 was of value to Schumann in bringing him to grips with the problems he was to face as a cyclic song composer— the relationship between piano and voice, symmetry of scale between songs and the sustaining of mood and character—and that we are fortunate incidentally to possess two or three of his best early songs by the way.

The most striking single feature of the cycle is its economy of texture, especially in the shorter songs. Just as a certain rapt sensuality is appropriate for the love-joy of the Heine songs in

Myrten, so *Liederkreis* proposes an altogether sparer, more neurotic language for situations where love or life is in question for any reason, and this discovery (one can certainly call it that in the context of Schumann's music) was to have far-reaching effects on later songs right up to the Mary Stuart cycle, op. 135. The tiny opening number of *Liederkreis*, 'Morgens steh' ich auf', is a case in point. Simple, almost too simple, in design, it has nevertheless some complexity of thought, imparted by the fidgety staccato accompaniment, the pauses at significant points of the setting, and the almost imperceptible asymmetry of the phrase-lengths, which Schumann achieves by carefully calculated word-repetitions. The sense of unease conveyed by these means remains in the mind for long after the rather plain melody is forgotten.

The second song, 'Es treibt mich hin', to another poem about anxious separation (now coupled with the prospect of reunion), employs similar devices. Again there are the impetuous changes of tempo, the staccato accompaniment and the unequal phrase-lengths. And in no. 4, 'Lieb' Liebchen', Schumann yet again uses a nervous staccato rhythm to impart a sense of emotional unrest, this time by following up Heine's ironic image of the beating heart as a carpenter hammering out the lover's coffin—a strange *volte-face* from 'Die Lotosblume'. It says much for the skill and aptness of the writing that these tiny songs, with their unremarkable folkish tunes, suffer nothing from the monotony of repeated imagery, especially as they also have melodic material in common. A particular aid to variety is some deft tone-painting. In 'Es treibt mich hin' the 'lagging hours' are suggested by a canon between voice and piano octaves, and the fair beloved by a melting five-note turn on to the dominant cadence, while in each verse of 'Lieb' Liebchen' the voice delays its last three notes as though reluctant to pronounce the sinister words *Totensarg* ('coffin') and *schlafen kann* ('can sleep'—i.e., the sleep of death):

'Es treibt mich hin' is also remarkable for being one of Schumann's earliest songs with a postlude based on new material, though 'Du bist wie eine Blume' is another. Several of the songs in *Dichterliebe* make use of this important device.

Just as one never hears the shorter *Dichterliebe* songs performed separately, so these three *Liederkreis* miniatures are hard to extract: they depend too much on the context they create for each other. Except for the chorale-like penultimate song, 'Anfangs wollt' ich'—a piece which is either enigmatic or derelict according to the singer's temperament—the others are all longer and more self-contained, but not always more successful. They include in fact some startling failures. One of these, 'Warte, wilder Schiffsmann', is little more than a hectic piano solo with added voice, prompted by one of Heine's rare outbursts (perhaps not wholly serious) of hair-tearing romanticism. The weak final song, 'Mit Myrten und Rosen', also leans heavily on a pianistic idea, as the prelude shows, the piano being reduced to chordal impotence as soon as the voice comes in with the tune. Schumann was naturally touched by the idea of a book of songs bearing messages of heartbroken love to the 'ferne Geliebte' (no doubt this is also the significance of the title of his op. 25). But he was dealing with an insipid poetic expression, and as in 'Lied der Suleika' it is the underlying quality of the poem—the truth or falseness of its feeling—which dictates the actual character of the music. Schumann's rare musical lies are almost always technical in origin. In for instance the fifth song of *Liederkreis*, 'Schöne Wiege meiner Leiden', Schumann blatantly overrides the point of the poem—the antithesis between the cradle of the first line and the grave of the last—by repeating Heine's first verse at the end to complete his rondo form. Curiously enough, the music appears to sense that it is on the wrong tack, for the dominant pedal and shortened conclusion filter out much of the character of what began as a beautiful and disturbing theme. Only in its restless, searching postlude does the song once more come to grips with the poem. The strophic 'Berg' und Burgen', though again full of restless charm, represents an even more abject surrender to musical convenience. Schumann must have realized that his music made no allowance for the cynical twist in the poem's final verse (where the river, like the beloved, is revealed in all her treachery) but was so lulled by the beauty of the scene—the rippling Schubertian waves, the boat drifting on the surface, the hazy Rheingau—that he understandably preferred not to come ashore.

By general consent the finest of the *Liederkreis* songs is 'Ich wandelte unter den Bäumen', and it is significant that in this wonderfully penetrating setting Schumann clearly modified during composition a form which began by being strophic. Heine's poem has four stanzas, and of these the first two and the last have the same music (slightly altered at the close), depicting the poet wandering listlessly through that same psychological woodland which Schumann was later to frequent in his Eichendorff songs. As in 'Die Lotosblume' the great moment of the song is a sudden key-change at about half-way, this time to introduce the birds, who seem to suggest that after all the poet's love is not hopeless. They do so to a new, deadly calm melody in the characteristic key of G major—the flattened submediant, which Schumann was often to use in his songs to suggest the idea of nature soothing the pains of humanity. The change back to B major is less telling, though psychologically the return of the opening music matches the poet's refusal to accept the proffered consolation, and at the end Schumann for once captures, by a simple repetition, the full force of Heine's self-pitying irony—'but I trust nobody'.

Towards the end of February 1840 Schumann's initial urge to set verse which he knew to be good rather than which personally attracted him shows signs of abating. From about this time date settings of artistically feeble but sympathetic poems by Chamisso and Julius Mosen. And also at this time Friedrich Rückert, a fine but fragile poet whose delicate lyrics clearly had a special appeal for Schumann, makes his bow. The Chamisso song 'Was soll ich sagen!' is of interest because it presents in reverse the same poet's *Frauenliebe und-leben* situation of a girl's total self-surrender to her husband. Musically its only interest is that it contains one of Schumann's not infrequent errors over word-stress, the poet's contrast of the old man's 'mein' and the girl's 'dein' being completely missed by the setting. 'Der Nussbaum', Schumann's only Mosen song, is another matter, and it fully merits its prominent place in *Myrten*. With considerable daring and resource the whole of an extended setting is derived from the piano's two-bar introduction with its suggestion of waving foliage and whispering blossom and (later in the poem) the girl's smiling, dream-laden sleep. The piano part is almost a *Fantasiestück* in its own right, but the vocal fragments, outlining the implied melody, are crucial to the effect of whispered confidences, and are a good example of why Schumann no longer felt the solo piano to be an adequate vehicle for his ideas.

The Rückert settings also include some masterly if insubstantial flower-songs. 'Jasminenstrauch', inexplicably left out of *Myrten*, is another example of Schumann's genius for catching the essence of a poetic idea and crystallizing it in a few seconds of unforgettable music. In this case the music is purely descriptive, but the style—folk-tune, aerial semiquaver accompaniment, and elusive chromatic harmonies—contains everything Schumann later required for the deeper insights of *Dichterliebe*.* Perhaps, on reflection, it was the first glimmering of such insights that made him prefer 'Aus den *Östlichen Rosen*' for *Myrten*: the elements are the same, except that flowers and their perfume have now become messengers of love or sorrow, so that the music is expressive as well as descriptive. In particular the subdominant harmony of the postlude, another Schumann fingerprint, has an air of regret for lost joys.

Not all the early Rückert songs are so perfectly poised between the image and its interpretation, and once balance has been lost the fall—in either direction—can be severe. Overstrained imagery is of course a recurrent feature of German romantic verse. It can be seen not quite at its worst in 'Zum Schluss', a poem which solves the problems of this life and the next in two brief, facile stanzas. Faced with such do-it-yourself philosophy, Schumann was apt to become pious, and although this hymn-like setting has a certain solemn charm as the concluding dedicatory number of *Myrten*, its value as an independent piece of music is almost nil. The same must be

---

* It also, less happily, suggested the setting of Wilhelmine Lorenz's 'Loreley'. The resemblances are almost tangible: tempo, rhythm, figuration, even the number of bars. But as Schumann himself wrote in another context, although 'two different readings of the same work are often equally good' (Eusebius), 'the original is generally better' (Raro).

said of the second 'Lied der Braut', whose solid chordal accompaniment proclaims the awe in which Schumann held the mother–daughter relationship which neither he nor Clara (whose parents separated when she was four) had ever truly experienced. The companion piece has admittedly more character, at least in the delicate piano part, but there is little in either song to reveal the future composer of *Frauenliebe und -leben*.

There remain two Rückert songs which stand apart from the rest, though in different ways. 'Volksliedchen' was Schumann's contribution to a Mozart commemoration album then in preparation (the song later appeared in 1850 as part of opus 51), and may have been written in conscious imitation of Mozart's 'folk' style (see for instance 'Das Veilchen'). It bears no conceivable resemblance to any actual folk-song; on the contrary its design is sophisticated almost to the point of contrivance, with irregularities of phrase introduced both by variations in word-stress (as in 'Schlusslied des Narren') and by short piano interludes (as in 'Freisinn'). The result, though not without charm, can seem too coy for comfort. By contrast 'Widmung', the dedicatory number of *Myrten*, is essentially a salon piece dignified to the level of high art by sheer directness of feeling. Rückert's poem, like Heine's 'Du bist wie eine Blume', is an uncomplicated expression of love and devotion, and for Schumann this inevitably meant a rich tapestry of diatonic harmony, as in the Heine flower-songs. Thus, although 'Widmung' sports the same flattened submediant relationship as 'Ich wandelte unter den Bäumen', there is no question of natural or supernatural calm as in the *Liederkreis* song, where the modulation was upwards by a minor sixth and so produced a tension between the brighter pitch and the darker tonality. In 'Widmung', Rückert's 'calm' and 'peace' are those of ordinary—or at any rate extraordinary—human companionship, so the music suggests profound warmth and repose by descending to the new key, E major, before reverting to the 'everyday' of A flat for a more or less straightforward reprise of the first verse.

Apart from Shakespeare, Chamisso, Mosen and Lorenz, five poets figure in isolated songs of this period—ranging from the minute and trivial 'Ein Gedanke' (Ferrand) which Schumann never released for publication,* and Hebbel's 'Sag' an, o lieber Vogel mein', to the important 'Aus den *Hebräischen Gesängen*', a setting of Byron's 'My Soul is Dark' from the *Hebrew Melodies*. The Byron song is the only one before 1849, and its depressive gloom strikes an odd, and disturbing, note among the lovesongs of *Myrten*. It remains, however, a source work for many later features of Schumann's style: the stylized harp writing of the *Wilhelm Meister* songs and the later Byron songs, opus 95, in most of which the instrument is associated with romantic melancholy; the evil winding quavers of 'Zwielicht' and 'Muttertraum'—both songs about the powers of darkness; and the introspective chromaticism of *Dichterliebe*. The mood is set by the piano introduction, where the main melodic interval is the semitone, and the harmony is dominated by the diminished seventh—the favourite romantic chord for suggesting gloom or distress of any kind—and unresolved dominant sevenths. This music:

returns twice in the course of the song: once as an interlude (before verse 2), and once in varied form as postlude, ending, however, on a major chord, as if Schumann were loath to allow depression the final word.† The voice part is unusually declamatory and tormented for its period. But the key phrase is in every sense the opening 'Mein Herz ist schwer', where the music sinks hopelessly on to an E minor cadence, from which keynote, despite desperate attempts, it never quite succeeds in escaping.

Schumann included in *Myrten* one other setting of a poem he believed to be Byron's, the 'Rätsel' of Catherine Fanshawe. The English poem is a clever and entertaining riddle on the letter

---

* It was published for the first time in *Musical Quarterly*, January 1942.

† There is later evidence of this same reluctance in the *Liederkreis* op. 39, *Dichterliebe* and the Lenau songs, op. 90.

H, but it inevitably loses much in Kannegiesser's German translation, and Schumann was not the composer to restore wit to a poem once it was lost. His treatment is heavy-handed, notably at the end, where he inserts an arch ('was ist's?') before giving the answer in musical terms (H is the German equivalent of musical note B). More genuinely witty are the two Venetian songs to poems by Thomas Moore, especially 'Wenn durch die Piazetta', whose music has a Mendelssohnian lightness and grace curiously lacking in Mendelssohn's own rather cumbersome setting of this poem. The other song, 'Leis' rudern hier', is a tender barcarolle which Schumann clearly conceived as a piano piece, for the words are fitted to the tune with little attention to their natural stresses or rhythms. Such errors of literary judgement occur fairly often throughout his songwriting, unfortunately not always redeemed by music of such irresistible charm.

3   The Cycles

Schumann's opening phase of song-writing ended in April 1840 with a visit to Berlin, where Clara was staying with her mother, Frau Bargiel. If correspondence with Clara absorbed his creative energies, being with her did so all the more, and no serious composition took place either during this Berlin trip or later, in June, when Clara came to Leipzig. In May they were again separated, and Robert's compensatory mechanism came into action with renewed vigour. By the 15th he had completed a second *Liederkreis*, this time of twelve Eichendorff settings, and was already at work on another Heine cycle, for which he composed twenty songs within about a fortnight. This cycle, reduced finally to sixteen numbers, was to be the *Dichterliebe*.

Schumann probably surprised himself with these two collections. Anxious as he was to justify himself as a composer of extended works, he would hardly have regarded a song-cycle as the fulfilment of that ambition, any more than in the 1830s he would have accepted a cyclic work like *Carnaval* as a substitute for a really successful sonata. Song was to be a prelude to greater things: to the opera he was already contemplating in March, or to choral works like *Paradise and the Peri*, success in which would give him a coveted place in the line of descent from Bach, Mozart, Beethoven and Mendelssohn. Fortunately his genius for miniatures was an itch which could not be left unscratched, and like a physical irritation it had the property of recurring for a time more strongly with each attempt to suppress it. There is no evidence that, in embarking on this second phase of lieder composition, he was thinking in terms of song-cycles (though internal evidence shows that such a plan preceded completion in the case of *Dichterliebe* at least). Rather did each song lead to the next as part of a normal creative process, with patterns emerging as Schumann's mind, and frame of mind, took hold of his material.

In the Eichendorff *Liederkreis*, op. 39, this impression is particularly strong, since although the songs are integrated in style and atmosphere there is no question of a circle or sequence of events in the strict meaning of the German word *Kreis*. At first sight the work is purely descriptive. We know, however, that Schumann composed these his first Eichendorff songs in a mood of high excitement after the Berlin holiday with Clara, an excitement enhanced by spring feelings and a natural inclination to project the beauty and promise of the season on to his own circumstances. So, from being a merely conventional simile for love, its joy and pain, nature suddenly acquired the force of a revelation. No longer did it seem necessary to point the significance of natural imagery: simply to evoke the image precisely and vividly was enough to convey the feeling by which it had been prompted. But Schumann was not the first artist to recognize that nature seen in this light had far greater potential as a symbol not just of feelings or ideas but of life in all its aspects. Eichendorff himself was something more than a landscape-painter, and his trees and streams comprise a forest that disturbingly suggests the labyrinth of antiquity—the symbol of a hostile world through which man wanders in fear surrounded by dark unknown powers. Of twelve songs in the final version of op. 39 no less than three have the significant word *Fremde*—strange or foreign country—in their titles. The woods may be a symbol by their endless growth of passing time, or by their permanence of the timelessness of God compared with human mortality. Time may stop completely in the forest but drag on elsewhere. And still, for the less troubled heart, woodland murmurs may be assurances of some longed-for happiness, with hope, like Fafner's blood, translating the sound according to our needs. In his first phase Schumann had explored this territory in isolated songs, notably 'Der Nussbaum' and 'Ich wandelte unter den Bäumen'. In neither song, however, is there the intensity of response to meaning in the environment that characterizes nine of the thirteen Eichendorff songs written during May. It is in fact an untopical feature of op. 39 that not only is nature frequently imagined as treacherous, menacing or downright hostile, but love as a source of bliss is largely ignored, while wedding processions twice appear as an image of transient joy. Schumann in his spring happiness had clearly not forgotten that spring is followed as well as preceded by winter.

The emotional range of the second *Liederkreis* is one of its great strengths, but it could not have been achieved without a corresponding enrichment of technique. Resourcefulness is a feature of both the first *Liederkreis* and *Myrten*—the resourcefulness of a composer who can find an answer to every problem though he may occasionally need an assumed style or expression to do so. The Eichendorff songs, by contrast, have the assurance of a technique tailored to its user's expressive needs, so that varied problems are solved without disparities emerging between this or that type of song, as they do in the more experimental Heine cycle. Opus 39 is notable for its stylistic as well as emotional and psychological unity.

The most obvious instance is the piano writing, and especially the use of accompaniment figures. Although such figures occur in the early songs they are by no means common. Indeed Schumann is known to have been wary of them, having only the previous year cautioned his younger contemporaries against a facile imitation of Schubert in this respect.* In opp. 24 and 25 his method is obviously that of a piano composer whose accompaniment mirrors each detail of the poem as closely as does the melody, while songs based on more or less continuous figuration—'Jasminenstrauch', 'Die Lotosblume'—are generally those where the idea expressed is either very simple or very static. In op. 39, however, the accompaniment offers a more generalized view of each poem. True, the piano part is still thematic and still comments by way of preludes, interludes, postludes and intermittent detail, but it no longer directs the argument as before. As a result a fuller relationship now develops between voice and piano, each with its own role which complements but does not duplicate the other's. For Schumann this was vital, since it released the piano from having, as it were, to sing the song, and made it available for all kinds of interior and ulterior emotional suggestion which was either absent from the verse or at best merely implicit in it.

In particular the emancipation of the piano brought with it a more richly embroidered keyboard fabric and increasingly articulate and sensitive harmonies. One has only to compare songs from phases 1 and 2—'Schöne Wiege meiner Leiden' with

---

* In an article on the composer Norbert Burgmüller, who had died in 1836 at the age of twenty-six.

'Waldesgespräch', 'Die Lotosblume' with 'Intermezzo', 'Aus den *Hebräischen Gesänge*' with 'Zwielicht'—to feel that in each case the later song uses the harmonic syntax in a more intuitive and versatile way. The syntax itself also shows signs of growing subtlety. For solo piano Schumann had developed a harmonic language of considerable flexibility, but of this there is little sign in the first songs, where a simple diatonicism prevails. In 'Schöne Wiege meiner Leiden', for instance, the principal melody is anchored firmly in E major, and the only 'foreign' notes, the three A sharps at the end, are pure tone painting with no harmonic function (the second episode, a more tortured passage full of diminished intervals, seems more adventurous, but again uses chromaticism mainly for the special effect of describing the poet's *Wahnsinn*, or mad frenzy). 'Waldesgespräch', by contrast, moves freely from E major through keys as remote as D sharp minor and C major, with no feeling of strain or artificiality. This new-found harmonic freedom comes to a head in 'Schöne Fremde', with its ambiguous opening, and the sinister 'Zwielicht', where chromatic effect crystallizes into a self-sufficient language of unexpected vividness and power.

Like the first *Liederkreis*, the second is linked by key sequence. In the first edition, published in 1842, the cycle began with a song called 'Der frohe Wandersmann' (republished in 1851 as one of the *Lieder und Gesänge*, op. 77), which is in D major as against the F sharp major of the concluding song, 'Frühlingsnacht'. For subsequent editions this rather hearty song in Schumann's open-air vein (cf. 'Freisinn') was replaced by the more retiring 'In der Fremde' (I) in F sharp minor, which thus introduces more satisfactorily what is otherwise a fairly tight circle of keys. Surprise plays its part in this design. It may for instance be easier to explain the logic of a transition to the second-inversion A major triad with which the second song, 'Intermezzo', begins from the D major of 'Der frohe Wandersmann' than from the F sharp major chord which closes 'In der Fremde' (I). But in performance the darkening effect produced by the change from A sharp to A natural beautifully enriches the lush harmonies of 'Intermezzo' in a way which the simple dominant modulation (tending as it does to brighten the sound) could hardly match.

Though not one of the great Eichendorff songs, 'In der Fremde' (I) sets the scene well enough with its melancholy folk-song tune, its rolling accompaniment figure and the mournful Neapolitan harmonies of its final bars. It also provides an interesting example of Schumann's fondness for rescanning his poets' lines to achieve rhythmic variety—a legitimate procedure which perhaps overreaches itself in such phrases as:

where the words are shoved into the tune regardless of their natural emphases. Another favourite surgical device, the repetition of the poet's first verse to complete a ternary form, is employed with powerful effect in 'Intermezzo', one of the few genuine love-songs in the collection. This wonderful piece, charged with a love-longing richer even than that of the Heine flower-songs in *Myrten*, depends for its effect on the tension built up by a syncopated accompaniment, an accelerating middle section, and a finely calculated movement from A major towards an exciting, even heroic D major, reverting suddenly to the security of the home key over a new, reassuring bass and with enriched harmonies. The effect would certainly be less if the return to A major accompanied fresh lines rather than a repeat of the opening 'dein Bildnis wunderselig'.

Harmonic movement of an even more graphic kind determines the shape of the Lorelei song 'Waldesgespräch'. The hero's key is a jovial E major, and Schumann makes a dramatic change to C major to suggest the enchanted maiden, unmasking her later in the song by the simple but effective device of repeating her theme in the home key. But there is contrivance at the end. Schumann is characteristically baffled how to render the poem's theatrical ending, and resorts to a stolid chordal figure in his ballad style, rounding the song off by an inapt repeat of the hero's prelude music, with its carefree jogging gait and picturesque suggestion of hunting horns. If 'Waldesgespräch' is a memorable song with architectural flaws, the next song, 'Die Stille', is a clever piece of work which perhaps lacks something in musical point. The comparison with Mendelssohn's setting, probably composed later, is instructive. Schumann's song, with its fluttering eyelashes, hesitant, lisping speech and trim figure, is a perfect cameo of the girl in the poem, where Mendelssohn's more elaborate and garrulous version might portray her mother (Mendelssohn makes almost a whole cabaletta out of 'I wish I were a bird'; Schumann, omitting one verse of the poem, captures in a tiny quatrain the volatile sentiment intended by the poet). And yet, though the expression is truthful, the music is diaphanous; it tells us too frankly that the girl, however charming, is feather-brained, a quality favoured in women of Schumann's day more than in those of our own.

This inconsequentiality in 'Die Stille' underlines the difficulty of rendering unmotivated happiness into memorable art: the feeling seems credible but trivial. Yet Schumann achieved near-miracles in this field when aided by vividly imagined verse, and the next two songs, 'Mondnacht' and 'Schöne Fremde', are both transcendent examples. One added quality is eroticism: in 'Mondnacht' the explicit image of sky and earth kissing in a haze of romantic moonlight; in 'Schöne Fremde' a less describable yet no less physical ecstasy again shrouded in a dream-like nocturnal vapour and faint shimmering light. Not the least of 'Mondnacht's' beauties is its simplicity of form, with—as in 'Der Nussbaum'—a single vocal phrase repeated several times as though hypnotized by the accompaniment. But the language is wonderfully subtle. For ten bars the music avoids a full-close cadence; then, as sky and earth meet, their kiss lasts for three bars of untrammelled E major—an effect of pure sensuality that even Wagner might have envied:

Schumann also handles well the resolution of this as a metaphor of man's search for peace and contentment. In the prelude the sense of quest might apply to the image or the imaged, but the postlude, with its conclusive harmonies, is an unambiguous extension of the poet's last line about the soul's homecoming.

Postlude and prelude combine similarly in 'Schöne Fremde', one of the best examples in Schumann of piano music throwing off an independent voice part which nevertheless retains its organic link with the accompaniment. In this poem, and the two which follow in Schumann's cycle, Eichendorff uses images of time—a ruined temple, a sleeping knight, an old castle—to enhance the atmosphere of strangeness and mystery. But in 'Schöne Fremde' Schumann is concerned only with the general mood: the forest, the dream, the ecstatic starlight. His excitement must have been intense, for the song is a seamless cloak, probably composed in essentials in a few minutes. 'Auf einer Burg' is more selfconscious. Here Schumann allows the poet's idea of a timeless forest and the river of life flowing past to direct his thoughts towards organ music and a slow procession. The song is modal with outlandish dissonances. But although the effect is haunting for the bearded knight in his tree-girt castle, the second verse's distant wedding flotilla seems to need some fresh musical idea rather than a simple repeat of the first. One explanation might be that Schumann regarded 'Auf einer Burg' and the next song, 'In der Fremde' (II), as a contrasting pair, the ambiguous final cadence of the one resolving into the clear A minor of the other. The songs share their main theme, and 'In der Fremde' (II) dwells on it too insistently for the link to have been entirely coincidental.

If this theme represents a verbal concept, it may be the passage of time. In 'Auf einer Burg' the process is slow, rhythmic, imponderable, like the ticking of some cosmic clock. 'In der Fremde' (II) is more anxious, using the ceaseless movement, rather than the eternal stillness, of the forest to convey fear and insecurity. The piano semiquavers babble through the undergrowth like a stream, sometimes visible, sometimes not; the voice theme twists and turns from tonic to dominant, uncertain of its direction; and as in 'Auf einer Burg', harmonic false relations suggest the strangeness and contradiction of past things glimpsed in or through a present context.

Thoughts of the past bring a sense of loss, and the realization that if the past has gone the present will go too—the despairing message of 'Zwielicht'. Schumann interpolated a song in complete contrast at this point, the Heine-like 'Wehmut' in E major, a piece of vocal piano music in the composer's early manner. Its function, however, seems to be that of offsetting the gloom, even cynicism, of the only three minor-key songs in op. 39 as first published, and we must regard 'Zwielicht' as the natural companion of 'Auf einer Burg' and 'In der Fremde' (II).

'Zwielicht' is an amazing work for an excitedly happy man to have composed, its message 'trust nobody, not even a friend, farther than you can see him'. In his daily life, Schumann was no cynic. Yet 'Zwielicht' shows that he knew the fears which breed cynicism, and how to translate them into music of unease and distrust. The language is that of twilit, fear-laden chromaticism (cf. 'Aus den *Hebräischen Gesängen*' and 'Muttertraum', both with the same winding accompaniment figure). But of equal importance is the changing rhythmic underlay of the four-times-repeated tune, the use of delayed stresses in verse 2 and quicker syncopations in verse 3, with a sudden decisiveness in the repeated chords and striding bass of the final verse, as the threat is made explicit. The vocal rhythm recalls 'Auf einer Burg' and has the same slow, relentless drive, but with a recitative-like hesitancy at the end, as though even the dark powers were not to be relied on.

This masterpiece of doubt is followed by another, though of a very different character. Eichendorff's 'Im Walde' parades all that is most joyous in life—marriage, birdsong, recreation —then banishes it as in 'Auf einer Burg', leaving only the darkness, the forest and the fear of oblivion. This time, however, Schumann confronts terror with hope. Although in his song, as in the poem, happiness is a fading dream, the voice clutching at its single motive as if at the faintest memory, the ending is tranquil with the idea of prayer uppermost. Since the key is a warm A major, we understand that fear, too, is transient and that what follows need not be a vacuum.

Schumann might have left it at that, but perhaps lacked the last degree of faith in spiritual things. He must, by his nature, journey home, and the brilliant 'Frühlingsnacht' proclaims his arrival. The woodland has now turned into a garden, and it tells us what we want to hear: that love is not after all dead and that life is secure. The change may be facile, but it meant a lot to Schumann, and 'Frühlingsnacht' is a song of impatient rapture equalled perhaps only by Schubert's 'Ungeduld'. As in 'Schöne Fremde' the piano is once again the main vehicle for the composer's excitement, and although the voice has a partially independent tune it is the accompaniment, with its throbbing semiquavers and flowing counter-melody, which dominates the song. The piano also, appropriately, has the last word. In the first half of the cycle postludes are the rule, but in the second there is only one of any length before 'Frühlingsnacht', in the untypical 'Wehmut'. The decisive piano solo which closes op. 39 may not compare for subtlety with the end of *Dichterliebe*, but its point is essentially the same. We feel that the composer has resolved his worst doubts, and can now face the future with a smile.

The *Liederkreis* virtually exhausted Schumann's interest in setting Eichendorff. Two further songs were composed late in 1840,* and years later poems by Eichendorff provided texts for half a dozen part-songs and for the solemnly impressive solo song 'Der Einsiedler'. Since most of the selected poems of op. 39 maintain some element of trauma or dark fantasy, it may be that Schumann came to associate Eichendorff with the uncertain months preceding his marriage, and later preferred to look elsewhere for romantic nature lyrics. A similar fate was Heine's. After the seventeen settings in the early phase, the addition in May of twenty more from the sixty-five poems of the *Lyrisches Intermezzo* meant that of the first eighty songs practically half were to poems by Heine. Yet with the single exception of 'Tragödie', Schumann never again set this poet, and indeed it would be surprising had he done so, for the ambiguities and ironies of 'Ich wandelte unter den Bäumen' or 'Wenn ich in deine Augen seh' ' or the sheer intensity of 'Die Lotosblume' would hardly have expressed the tender togetherness of his early married life, while later his taste was increasingly for a sententiousness into which Heine seldom strayed. Without stretching the relationship between an artist's life and his work beyond acceptable limits, one may conclude that

---

* 'Der Schatzgräber' and 'Frühlingsfahrt', op. 45, nos. 1 and 2.

Dichterliebe, like the earlier Heine songs, is necessarily the work of a composer in urgent love rather than the settled family man Schumann became in September 1840. Indeed the very title proclaims as much. Whereas the earlier collections had titles of a picturesque generic nature, the word *Dichterliebe* sets up altogether more specific resonances—the idea, already proposed in 'Mit Myrten und Rosen', of the poet enshrining in verse his (by implication) tragic and unrequited love. By May, of course, Schumann's was neither. But he was still experiencing the nervous strain of parting and reunion which, coupled with less happy memories of times not so long past, was well able to induce that sense of heightened awareness so inseparable from the idea of romantic love.

In fact *Dichterliebe* is not strictly a tragic cycle in the sense of Schubert's *Die Winterreise* or *Die schöne Müllerin*, which end respectively in madness and suicide. Schumann's final song, 'Die alten, bösen Lieder', is an act of renunciation culminating in acceptance and aching tranquillity. Also absent from *Dichterliebe* is the feeling of narrative (albeit largely implicit) which Schubert retained from Müller's cycles. Schumann's subject is, so to speak, the life and death of an emotion, and although we may choose to regard the only narrative song, 'Ein Jüngling liebt ein Mädchen', as a capsule version of what has happened to the poet, our understanding of the music does not depend on such an interpretation. All we need know is that the poet has loved and lost, that he feels himself to have been wronged, but that (as the flowers seem to say in 'Am leuchtenden Sommermorgen') the truth is simpler and more innocent. Heine's poems, which include several of his finest short lyrics, catch vividly the unforgettable moments of love: the thrill of avowal, the joy of physical contact, the first pain of distrust, the agony of loss and the deadness of its acceptance. But it is Schumann's music which binds these moments into a total experience, a real-life affair examined from within. And if the conclusion is not necessarily one he would have reached in his own life, that was personally his good fortune and artistically ours.

Today *Dichterliebe* strikes us as the most realistic of love-song cycles, the one which most faithfully reflects the everyday things of love and its usual everyday conclusion. For this

Heine's poetry must take a good deal of credit. Its complete lack of bombast or extravagance, its sparing and always pointed use of metaphor, its formal simplicity, added to the usual Heine fingerprints of irony and disillusion—all these qualities have a truth undiminished by the technical virtuosity which goes into their blending. Heine was unusual among German poets of his day in understanding the mechanism of implication. A poem like 'Im wunderschönen Monat Mai', for instance, depends for its undeniably mournful effect almost entirely on what is *not* stated, while the text itself contains no hint of non-requital except possibly in the last line, 'mein Sehnen und Verlangen', and even this is capable of other interpretation. Such hidden suggestion has untold value to a composer, for word-setting is much more the art of completing the incomplete than of ornamenting the complete. Schumann's best early Heine songs had already shown how, without violating the simple, economical character of poems like 'Lieb' Liebchen' or 'Du bist wie eine Blume', music could bring undercurrents of meaning to the surface and project them as a new dimension of the poetry. In *Dichterliebe* this technique is carried a stage beyond, via the work's semi-narrative structure, which allows still further implications to be drawn from suitably selected poems. Thus, to take an extreme example, the seventeen-bar 'Aus meinen Tränen spriessen' is ideally heard on four different levels: the surface simplicity of the poem itself, which Schumann expresses by an apparently bland tune of only six different notes in the metre of the verse; a surface level of uncertainty within the tune itself, suggested by the avoidance of the keynote (A) in favour of the mediant (C sharp) and supertonic (B), on which note no less than three of the song's four vocal lines, including the last, end; a still deeper layer of doubt in the accompanying harmonies, not only the chromatics of line 3, but also the ambiguous first chord (A major or F sharp minor), the dark subdominant harmonies in the last line, and the little sighing phrase by which, almost as an afterthought, the piano resolves the discord on which the tune ends; and finally the deep level of context, set by the preceding song, 'Im wunderschönen Monat Mai', which has already made fruitful use of the A major–F sharp minor antithesis.

Most of these points are harmonic, and indeed harmony is the most important expressive device throughout *Dichterliebe*. With few exceptions the tunes, taken on their own, are of surpassing simplicity, just as Heine's poems are often couched in almost childishly straightforward terms. Yet the listener is hardly ever aware of this since, as in 'Aus meinen Tränen spriessen', not only do the tunes themselves carry undertones of harmonic meaning, but the piano invariably adds its own comment. As in op. 39 the accompaniments are much more figure-prone than in most of the earlier songs. But whereas the *Liederkreis* figuration tends to be pianistic in conception, either chordal or in some other way textural, many of the *Dichterliebe* songs use figures conceived as counter-melodies, linear in character and producing a generally transparent texture. From a harmonic point of view this is the more flexible method, as we hear at once in 'Im wunderschönen Monat Mai':

or later in the brilliant 'Das ist ein Flöten und Geigen', simply because it allows more harmonic activity. Spare textures can also, as we saw in the earlier Heine songs, suggest an atmosphere of mental tension which specially suits *Dichterliebe*—a cell-by-cell probing of the nervous system quite different from the undergrowth analogies of the Eichendorff songs, where luxuriating growths of sound stand for what is essentially a fantasy world. Fantasy, or to be more precise dreams, certainly play an important part in the later stages of *Dichterliebe*, but they are always dreams from which the sleeper awakes to a painful reality before the song is over—dreams, in fact, recounted in a waking state and seen for the delusions they are.

With simple melody acting as a framework for subtleties of harmony and texture, one looks also for similar tensions in the field of rhythm, and indeed they are not hard to find. Rhythm in the wider sense—that is, phrase-structure—had always been a blind spot of Schumann's, especially in song, where it was too easily dominated by verse-metre. Schumann could get round the difficulty by ignoring the poet's scansion (as in 'Die Stille'), or by repeating words or lines, or by breaking the metre up with piano interludes. Alternatively he could, in shorter songs at least, use a natural squareness of phrase as an expressive device against which any variation would set up tensions which could themselves be controlled within fine limits. In fact no less than nine of the sixteen songs in *Dichterliebe* follow the verse-metre exactly. In the seven songs where it is varied the process is conscious and functional, and in the two where it is unexpectedly unvaried (the last two in the cycle) there are again special factors at work. The cycle opens, in fact, with two songs of a straightforward metrical cut (they are also the first two poems of Heine's collection; after the fourth, Schumann departs from Heine's sequence). 'Im wunderschönen Monat Mai', the song of avowal, is effectively strophic, and has a tune of almost reckless plainness which, however, ends remarkably in the subdominant (of A major, that is: the tune is always in that key). This delicate touch might not in itself drop any dark hints but for the highly equivocal prelude and postlude, which vacillate between A major and F sharp minor, finally opting for the dominant of F sharp. 'Aus meinen Tränen spriessen' follows this with its own blend of the naive and the ambiguous, so that after only two songs (forty-three bars of music) the poet's innocent professions of love have already cast shadows over a happy thought. The third song, 'Die Rose, die Lilie', contains no such forebodings, and has been considered incongruous, without its obvious perfection being questioned. But it fits the context. The poet's subconscious fears have been conveyed to us, and perhaps also, at the conscious level, to him. But he need not yet admit to himself that he is anything but excitedly happy, and this mood 'Die Rose, die Lilie', with its agitated accompaniment and breathless vocal dactyls, conveys exactly. Listening to it in the cycle, we sense an irony, and Schumann perhaps acknowledges this by ensuring that the only modulation is towards the dark subdominant.*

However, if the poet of 'Die Rose, die Lilie' is self-deceiving, 'Wenn ich in deine Augen seh'' brings awareness with a vengeance. This time the context warns us that the girl's 'ich liebe dich' is itself deceitful (it might at best mean: 'ich liebe dich, und Hans, und Karl, und Adolf'), and the tears this prompts make a perfect instance of *Stimmungsbrechung*. To that effect Schumann once more uses the subdominant, both for the song's key (G in relation to the preceding D major), again during the song, and in the lovely postlude, where the harmonies weep for the sad sweetness of such love. The song also uses gentle dissonance to prefigure pain, on 'Brust', 'Himmelslust', and the crucial words 'sprichst' and 'liebe':

and what one might call rhythmic dissonance, with imperceptibly unequal phrase-lengths diagnosing an unsteady pulse. The poet can now no longer doubt his misfortune, and the fifth song, 'Ich will meine Seele tauchen', is a last wistful glance back to vanished pleasures—the first song unequivocally in a minor key. It has two tunes (one each in voice and piano, both

---

* On the poem's last line. Schumann ends with a one-and-a-half-line repeat, to allow him to fill out his tune from Heine's exiguous lyric.

perfectly symmetrical), and a tremulous accompaniment figure inspired perhaps by the quiver of the remembered kiss, or by the liquid word *Kelch* ('chalice'). In the postlude, in either case, the demisemiquavers flow once again as tears, beneath gloomy chromatic harmonies.

The mood changes abruptly for 'Im Rhein, im heiligen Strome'. The key is still minor, but with the stern magnificence of Cologne Cathedral and the majestic Rhine dwarfing the misery and fickleness of mankind. In both the first verse and the long postlude Schumann is concerned mainly with the *mise-en-scène*, and the piano's Handelian dotted rhythms superbly suggest the heavy wash of the river as well as the organ-playing from inside the cathedral. In between is a mellower passage in sixths and thirds, the image of the beloved in the madonna, darkened momentarily, in a stab of remembrance, by a sudden switch from G to E flat in the piano part. But it is the grandeur of the scene which stays in the poet's mind, as the seventh song, 'Ich grolle nicht', shows. This famous piece is one of Schumann's literary travesties. But the transformation of Heine's genuinely self-effacing poem into a song of passionate and bitter resentment was clearly deliberate, and is so effective that one must adopt the poet's stance and not complain. The change is accomplished with the simplicity of genius: a few over-protesting repeats of *ich grolle nicht* ('I bear no grudge'), a rising note of anger in the voice, the piano's hammered chords finally dismissing the whole affair in a perfunctory C major cadence, and the poet's forgiveness becomes the composer's moral superiority. Even the most baritonal performers should risk the final top A, an afterthought on Schumann's part, but the only musical line.

'Ich grolle nicht' is the public side of the poet's grief. The next three songs, all in minor keys each the subdominant of the last, are its private, personal expression. The desolate 'Und wüssten's die Blumen' is again strophic (written out, as always in *Dichterliebe*) using repetition to deepen the sense of traumatic bewilderment, and harmonic movement to remind us that the agony is not without its sweetness, a point underlined by the hint of A major in the varied fourth verse, where the poet seems to take morbid pleasure in the incommunicability of his misery. But typically the sting is in the tail. 'Only she knows my sorrow, because she it is who caused it.' So, after a bitter vocal cadence, the piano wells up into a postlude based on new and more indignant material:

which then carries over, much varied, into 'Das ist ein Flöten und Geigen', where it provides the right-hand accompaniment:

Spiritually the cycle now reaches its nadir. The poet imagines his beloved's wedding to another man, and, as in 'Der arme Peter', the situation provokes a sardonic waltz, with flute, violin and drum much in evidence. Though it feels like a single flash of inspiration, this song is assembled as meticulously as a wristwatch. There are four verses alternating between tonic and subdominant, each verse formed by a couplet from the poem with one line repeated to make an uneven grouping of three phrases. The effect of the odd third phrase, always on a falling gradient, is despairing in the extreme, not least because the piano meanders on, sourly oblivious of the poet's troubles, until in the coda even the angels' weeping sounds ironic. Such bitterness is inconsistent with sanity, so in the next song, 'Hör ich das Liedchen klingen', tears again fulfil their proper function of relieving mental agony. This time Schumann uses a simple symmetrical tune to conjure up a dazed reminiscence of one sung by the beloved, jogging the singer's memory with hesitant suggestions in the piano introduction. The accompaniment unambiguously portrays weeping. But in the postlude there is a further recollection of the tune, and a moment of protest before the futility of the situation overcomes all resistance. The closing bars are among the saddest in the whole lieder repertoire.

The cycle now moves towards its conclusion, via objectivity and dream-waking symbolism to the renunciation of 'Die alten, bösen Lieder', which is also the final poem of the *Lyrisches Intermezzo*. Objectivity is represented by the pseudo-folksong 'Ein Jüngling liebt ein Mädchen', a kind of cautionary tale in which the futility of love suddenly loses its inferences of personal tragedy and becomes just another fact of life. Heine's dry conciseness is as usual ironic, but for the irony in Schumann's song we need to refer again to the context, which tells us that the offbeat stresses in the piano part must be treated as over-emphases, the squareness of the vocal phrases as mock-ingenuousness, and the sudden harmonic clouding of the last line as hysterical. Taken at its face value, this song would have no place in *Dichterliebe*. But as before, irony gives way to consolation: then, in 'Hör ich das Liedchen klingen', it was the balm of unrepressed tears; now, in 'Am leuchtenden Sommermorgen', it is the imagined sympathy of nature —Ruskin's 'pathetic fallacy'—which soothes both injury and resentment. For this, significantly, the music brightens to the dominant (B flat), the change being effected by a German sixth progression, which not only establishes the new key, but also prepares the way for subsequent 'modulations' to B major and G major. If we are to believe his innocent song, the poet has at last found peace of mind. But the piano still sheds tears, and although the flowers speak calmly in Schumann's peace-with-nature key, G major (cf. 'Ich wandelte unter den Bäumen'), their voices darken for the apparent moment of truth: 'du trauriger, blasser Mann'. A deeper truth, however, points out that the flower speech is imaginary, that the will to forgive comes from within, and that the poet's love has therefore lost its power to wound. All this emerges from the beautiful postlude, a characteristic piece of Schumann piano writing in which a new and unforgettable theme rises from the delicate tracery of arpeggios—a distillation in music of tranquillity won by suffering. Four songs later, the same music forms a completely apt conclusion to the cycle.

But first there is need for subconscious as well as conscious acceptance. Often, says Heine, when we think we have forgotten pain, we dream of the past and pain returns. Schumann's next three songs are all dream-haunted, though in each the pain is less, until the dream is no more than a reverie, blowing in the wind. 'Ich hab' im Traum geweinet' is more than that, a trauma also in the Greek sense. Heine's poem suggests a paradox which is apparent rather than real when it relates three different dreams, one of the beloved's death, another of her infidelity, and a third of her fidelity, after each of which the poet wakes up in tears. The actual loss is, after all, total in any case. Schumann observes this point in music of almost melodramatic starkness, in the remote key of E flat minor. The voice starts alone on the B flat of the previous song, and for two verses the piano merely punctuates this monologue with dry, brittle chords in the bass register. Then for the final verse, the dream of continuing love, the two come together in a last elegy for lost joy, with rending discords to accompany the moment of awakening. The next dream-song, 'Allnächtlich im Traume', is more elusive, and musically one of the cycle's more ambiguous movements. The memory is already fading, and even the poet can no longer recall his dream exactly—except for the cypress frond, a symbol of mourning. The song, therefore, is restless with syncopated rhythms and unequal phrase-lengths, but not unhappy in its bright B major. At the end, where the strophic form is slightly varied to accommodate the idea of waking, the music perfectly expresses the poet's frustrating inability to remember what the beloved said to him, but hardly suggests that it matters a great deal.

The third dream-song, 'Aus alten Märchen winkt es', has an almost childlike quality, as the poet's gaze turns away from the past out towards an imaginary land of delight and heart-ease. The poem is more elaborate than most in the *Lyrisches Intermezzo*, and full of musical ideas which Schumann seizes on gratefully for one of his most evocative and colourful songs—a pageant of elfin horns, magic flickering lights, and dancing fairies (it is the idea of a dance which seems to have conditioned the comparatively square rhythms of the setting). The first part of the song portrays the dance, but at the words 'if only I could go there' Schumann holds the theme back in augmentation as this vision, too, begins to elude him; and where the dance has been characterized by brilliant diatonic harmonies, the outlines now gradually fade into a blurred chromaticism, leaving only a last brief memory of dreamland in the postlude.

As the sun rises on this last dream-fantasy, so it sets finally on the poet's love: take these terrible songs and visions, he sings in 'Die alten, bösen Lieder', and sink them in the ocean. Both in Heine's poem and in Schumann's song there is more than a touch of self-ridicule in this idea—a sardonic grandiosity tailored to a once-held view of the affair's importance—and the music responds impressively to all Heine's exaggerated images of weight, size and squareness, the huge coffin and bier, the twelve giants to carry them, and the vastness of the watery grave. But the end of *Dichterliebe* is not to be found in Heine. It was, as we have seen, not Schumann's nature to conclude such a work on an ironic note, and instead he turns the irony against itself with music which retorts that the love did indeed count for much, and that in terms of experience it still does. The change of heart is beautifully accomplished in harmonic terms. As the coffin slips below the surface to an uneasy piano *ostinato* on a dominant seventh of F sharp, the music suddenly clears in relief, moves briefly into D major for Heine's last couplet about the burial of his love and pain, and then settles into a heartfelt D flat, the tonic major of the song and the dominant of the key in which the cycle opened, for its postlude. This is an extended version (almost a piano piece in its own right) of the postlude to 'Am leuchtenden Sommermorgen', and although it embraces new material its point is essentially that of the earlier song. We may, with Heine, rid ourselves of the past and its impedimenta, but not of the experience or (fortunately) of the peace gained at such cost. Perhaps Schumann was lucky that a repeat he would have made anyway happened to work so well in literary terms. When he tried the device later, in *Frauenliebe und -leben*, it remained at the level of contrivance.

As well as the sixteen numbers of *Dichterliebe*, Schumann set four other poems from the *Lyrisches Intermezzo* intending them for inclusion in the cycle. With one exception they are inferior to any in the published collection, and were no doubt excluded either for this reason or because they could not be fitted into the work's psychological plan. The only one which might have had a place for pure musical quality is 'Dein Angesicht', a ternary-form song in the amorous style of 'Intermezzo'. In Heine's collection the poem follows the opening four (which Schumann set in sequence), but its enigmatic talk of death has no relevance to *Dichterliebe* at this point, while its form and idiom lack the intensity for a place later in the cycle. 'Dein Angesicht' was published in 1854 as part of op. 127, which also includes another *Dichterliebe* reject, 'Es leuchtet meine Liebe', an unashamed piano scherzo with interpolated voice part, much indebted to Mendelssohn. The other two discarded items, 'Lehn' deine Wang'' and 'Mein Wagen rollet langsam', appeared posthumously in 1858 among the four songs, op. 142. 'Lehn' deine Wang'' is in scale and design more the *Dichterliebe* type of song, but its passion is curiously rhetorical, and although the piano triplets lend impetus the vocal line is patently contrived. 'Mein Wagen rollet langsam', though it would have cut a strange figure in *Dichterliebe*, is much the more interesting of these two songs. The poem, concise, vivid and enigmatic, is true to Heine's early lyric style, but Schumann—who had recently completed two long coach journeys for Clara's sake—responded mainly to the pictorial imagery, the rolling carriage-wheels and the poet's musing about his beloved. In fact so dominant are these ideas that their musical equivalents stretch the song to about twice its natural length, including no less than twenty-eight amiable bars of postlude (out of seventy-three) after Heine's figmental intruders have evaporated.

Soon after the completion of *Dichterliebe* (the final fair-copy is dated 1 June), Clara returned from Berlin, and once again Schumann's creative energies were diverted. Not until July did songs flow again from his pen, for the last time before his marriage in September. The less well-known compositions from this month and the next include settings of Reinick and Geibel and of translations by Chamisso from the Danish of Hans Andersen and the French of Pierre Béranger. But it is the settings of original peoms by Chamisso which have acquired fame alongside *Dichterliebe* in the form of the similarly constituted cycle *Frauenliebe und -leben*.

In the earlier cycle Schumann had described the pain and disillusionment of misdirected love as understood by any man of sensitivity (the implication of the word *Dichter*). *Frauenliebe und -leben* attempts a woman's view of another kind of love— that which is reciprocated, has its proper growth in marriage and children, and its inevitable end in separation by death. In design the works have something in common. In each the emotional drama is sketched in a series of tableaux, like still frames from a cinefilm, and from each a sequence of events, though not described, can be inferred. Technical similarities are also significant: the careful use of key-sequence, the importance of the accompaniment and especially of piano postludes and figuration, and not least Schumann's extraordinary flair for catching in music the precise spirit of the words he set. But comparisons should not be pressed too far. Most of them could apply to almost any of Schumann's song collections. Whatever else they may do, Chamisso's poems give little insight into the real nature of female love, for the good reason that their author was a male writing not in an attempt to comprehend but at the behest of an ideal of feminine subservience shared by many men in the early 1800s (including writers greater than Chamisso, as Dickensians will not need reminding). At best the poems give an elegant view of how the more authoritarian paterfamilias hoped to be regarded by his wife, and particularly how he assumed she would greet his death. From Schumann's point of view it was a more serious fault that the cycle's heroine is so self-abasing as to be vacuous, and therefore unresponsive to the kind of musico-psychological treatment which is one of the great features of *Dichterliebe*.

In fact the artist in Schumann perceived this immediately, and the style of *Frauenliebe und -leben* is much simpler than that of the earlier cycles. More than in any of his previous songs he pinned his faith on melody, and the tunes in *Frauenliebe und -leben* are not only broader than those elsewhere, they are also shapelier and in some cases more grateful to sing. Harmonically, however, the songs are dull. Mostly they remain anchored to the home key, avoiding even those modulations which present themselves in the natural course of the melodic line, and then in desperation moving into a new key so deliberately as to destroy all sense of surprise or freshness. One rather odd consequence of this is that many of the songs tend to sound the same. Almost all of them owe something to Beethoven's *An die ferne Geliebte*, though Schumann also drew heavily on the *Myrten* style of 'Widmung', a song clearly imitated in *Frauenliebe und -leben* by 'Helft mir, ihr Schwestern'. Finally, the piano writing is by far the most narrowly conceived of any in Schumann's 1840 cycles, not excluding the musically more uneven Heine *Liederkreis*. Most of the accompaniments are in some way or at some stage chordal, and in particular repeated quaver chords become something of a mannerism, turning up in no less than four of the eight songs. To modern ears this type of writing is apt to sound hymnic, though the intended effect is perhaps a sense rather of sweetness, purity and self-effacing nobility than of any specific piety. Within these limits the piano is important as always, and although significant preludes are lacking, all but one of the eight songs have substantial postludes, sometimes punctuated by short vocal repeats.

The first song, 'Seit ich ihn gesehen', is quick to establish a devotional mood, with its clean, middle-register harmonies and slow triple time, strongly reminiscent of the start of *An die ferne Geliebte*. Like the equivalent song in *Dichterliebe* it has two verses set strophically, with a piano postlude reverting to the music of the opening. But whereas in 'Im wunderschönen Monat Mai' the effect was one of puzzlement and ambiguity, here it suggests certitude and a feeling of contemplation, the music barely straying at all from B flat major, in an almost embarrassing likeness of the lowly maid confronted for the first and last time by true love. The second song, 'Er, der Herrlichste von allen', elaborates her feelings: 'He is the finest of men, perfect in all respects; I must rejoice to be able so much as to look at him, for I am nothing and he deserves everything.' The setting is extended into a rondo by a concluding repeat of Chamisso's first verse, and the accompaniment risks monotony with its insistent repeated chords and triadic E flat harmonies. But an unforgettable melody, leaping in sincere exultation, saves the day—as Schumann clearly recognized, for we hear it four times. As so often, subdominant harmony figures prominently in the song's later stages, but in place of the yearning effect produced in *Dichterliebe* it now expresses complacency and even finality, until in the postlude a more hesitant, chromatic strain rightly questions the aptness of those qualities. For the next song, 'Ich kann's nicht fassen', Schumann introduces a further ambiguity which is not strictly present in Chamisso. To her boundless amazement the girl's love is reciprocated, and she expresses her surprise in formal terms of disbelief. The music, however, while echoing her tremulous excitement, also suggests by its uneasy minor key and urgent piano chords that doubt really does exist. Other passages depict her slumbrous bliss at the mere thought of such happiness. But the song ends sadly, with a postlude (for voice and piano) based on a lovely variant of the main theme and a repeat of the poem's incredulous opening. It is perhaps the most unexpected and touching effect in the cycle.

Having reached the subdominant relative minor of the cycle (C minor) for its moment of uncertainty, the music now brightens into E flat again and thence back to B flat. Not only in key, but also in form and harmony 'Du Ring an meinem Finger' recalls 'Er, der Herrlichste von allen'; it even lapses into the same repeated chords as the excitement mounts to the climax on 'angehören ganz', the moment of supreme self-giving; places the same dependence on its admittedly fine melody; and makes the same complacent move towards the subdominant in the postlude. The cycle itself continues in the other direction, to the home key of B flat for the day of fulfilment—the wedding-day. 'Helft mir, ihr Schwestern' is lively and gay, yet also squarely cut and contrived in effect, with the devout repeated chords replacing the 'Widmung' figure at mention of the lord and master, and a moment of sheer falseness as the music darkens perfunctorily to G flat for the heroine's 'sad farewell' to her sisters:

This time the postlude is a bridal march, so like the one Wagner later composed for *Lohengrin* that one is tempted to assume a subconscious link between the two.

The next poem, 'Süsser Freund', is Chamisso's version of the 'little stranger' episode, and it is perhaps not surprising that Schumann, who had not yet won his own bride, was no more than conventionally touched by this first intimation of parenthood. The song is ternary in form, and the slowest-moving in the cycle, though with the inevitable quaver chords for the faster middle section, where the heroine apostrophizes her remarkable husband. In the recitative-like outer sections both word-setting and harmony have a mechanical air, and it is sad to hear the composer of *Dichterliebe* moving from the dominant of G major to C major via a copybook sequence of dominant sevenths. 'An meinem Herzen', which celebrates the patter of tiny feet as forecast by 'Süsser Freund', uses even more restricted harmonies, yet has an undeniable freshness, even wit, its pace increasing with the mother's excitement while in a suave postlude the child sleeps on oblivious of the stir he has created. Though not Schumann at his most inspired, the music has fine aptness to both poetry and situation.

Before the last song, 'Nun hast du mir den ersten Schmerz getan', we understand the death of the husband (whether or not prematurely is unclear). The short poem is set as an in tempo recitative in D minor, rather grand and censorious in style—Dido rebuking Aeneas. But its tone gradually softens with the heroine's vow to live on in the memory of her past love, while the music brightens aptly towards the dominant. Then, with a magical switch to the dominant of B flat, we are back in the music of the first song, a change which, though effective and superficially justified by the poem's last line ('there I have you and my lost happiness, you my world') is an odd comment on the character's mental growth from the innocent maid of 'Seit ich ihn gesehen'. One is tempted to suggest that the comment is not altogether inapt. But Schumann's procedure is in any case primarily a musical convenience, and lacks the penetrating significance of the postlude to *Dichterliebe*.

It would be misleading to see in *Frauenliebe und -leben* evidence of a decline in Schumann's creative faculty so soon after the great works of May. In its fashion it reflects Chamisso's verse as faithfully as the *Liederkreis* reflects Eichendorff's or *Dichterliebe* Heine's. But Schumann was the wrong composer to set inferior verse, for his literary antennae were too sensitive, too perceptive, and where a Schubert or a Brahms could make great songs from weak poetry by ignoring what was irrelevant to their needs, Schumann could not, in honesty, work in this way. A poet himself, he understood too well the mechanics of poetry. Nor could he bring taste to his rescue, for his taste was palpably unreliable. Unlike Schubert, he was always prepared to justify his choice on literary as well as musical grounds, and this meant that Kerner was Mörike's equal, or Chamisso Heine's, or Kulmann Rückert's—always the personal factor betraying sound judgement. Had he shared Wolf's powers of discrimination, we might have had a larger number of fine songs from his pen. Alternatively the great songs we have might have been smaller, less personal, and therefore less perceptive. The loss of *Dichterliebe* or the Eichendorff songs would have been a heavy price to pay for however many 'Talismanes' or 'Freisinns'.

4 *Autumn*

Apart from the earlier 'Was soll ich sagen!', Schumann's Chamisso songs can all be assigned with fair certainty to July–August 1840, the period of *Frauenliebe und -leben*. They include, in fact, only one other setting of an original poem by Chamisso. The rest are of translations by him from Béranger, Hans Andersen, and 'the modern Greek',* poems naturally quite varied in content and character. Not surprisingly, there is no echo of the mood of *Frauenliebe und -leben*. Taken as a group together with the contemporary Geibel settings of opp. 30 and 51, they are the most ambitious songs Schumann composed in 1840, and suggest that having demonstrated his mastery of the tiny lyric form he was eager to prove himself with a larger canvas and in a more dramatic style. He seems to have sensed that to achieve this he would need to cultivate a more detached view of his subject-matter. In *Dichterliebe* and *Frauenliebe und -leben*, as well as in the great majority of the earlier collected songs, the personal impression is all-important. Even in an apparently descriptive song like 'Auf einer Burg' the scene is transfigured into an expression of feeling to which details of landscape, character and drama are incidental. From now on, however, Schumann's songs partake increasingly of the nature of theatre, and the more intimate lyric style occurs both less frequently and less successfully.

For the composer of 'Belsatzar' and 'Die beiden Grenadiere', the ballad was an obvious first choice as a vehicle for objective description, and two of the three Chamisso songs, op. 31, are of this type. The first, 'Die Löwenbraut', is a straightforward narrative with dramatic *dénouement*; the second, 'Die rote Hanne', is more in the nature of a student song with verses and refrains set for optional chorus. It would be hard to decide

---

* Chamisso's own claim for the German text of 'Verratene Liebe'. Sams (*op. cit.*) suggests that the real source was Fauriel's *Chants populaires de la Grèce moderne* (1825).

which is the greater failure. The earlier ballads, though hardly dramatic, are strong in atmosphere and imaginative in detail, and show how even from uncongenial verse-types Schumann could usually extract enough music to sustain interest for the length of the song, given the slightest narrative appeal. But the most rabid leomane might baulk at the portrait of a lion so devoted as to kill his mistress and allow himself to be shot rather than see her married against her will. Schumann's setting, with its interminable slow *ostinati*, respectful, four-square phraseology, and hopelessly funked climax (reminiscent of the feeble ending to 'Belsatzar'), is no better and no worse than the poem deserves. 'Die rote Hanne', one of the two Béranger translations, is perhaps a more surprising failure, for its story of the ugly red-head who finally discovers contentment as the wife of a poacher is not without a certain sententious charm. The stumbling-block for Schumann is the refrain, half-pious, half-ironic, which squares the verses off dully and prompts a chorale-like treatment fatal to any rhythmic or melodic interest. Incidentally these two songs share a curious trademark with other ballads by Schumann: the main theme which opens with a leap (usually upwards) from dominant to tonic. The piano introduction of 'Die rote Hanne' recurs only a little altered in another Schumann ballad of this year, 'Blondels Lied'.

The remaining song of op. 31, 'Die Kartenlegerin' (the girl who tells fortunes with cards) has nothing much in common with its companions apart from a somewhat noncommittal manner, a cool sense of observed reality as against personal, emotional statement. The girl of the title is not a professional clairvoyant, but a bored seamstress who reaches for the cards whenever her mother falls asleep. The poem, another translation from Béranger, portrays her as something of a soubrette, sharp-witted, good-humoured, and of course much too practical to pay serious attention to what the cards predict. Thus the song, too, treats the whole thing as a game. As the girl chatters gaily to herself, so Schumann finds a charmingly negligent melody (over fluttering piano chords on and off the beat) which recurs like a rondo theme, with a couple of mock-tragic episodes for the cards' less attractive predictions. The sketch is telling and likeable if not musically out of the ordinary, and, in particular, it shows how quick Schumann was to respond to essential qualities in a poem, even when no directly personal experience was involved.

Certainly nothing could be farther in spirit from the allusive fantasy-world of op. 39 or the intense emotion of *Dichterliebe*. The new style is essentially matter-of-fact, its melodic idiom a colloquial one based, like everyday speech, mainly on commonplaces, while the piano lightly touches in the sort of detail—tone of voice, facial expression—which in ordinary conversation influences our reaction to what is said. Such writing, which sets a higher premium on pure observation than on emotion, is rare in Schumann, though common in Schubert, who remained enough of a classicist to be able to see the world as something apart from himself. Schumann could usually do this only by default, when his feelings were not engaged by a poem, and in such cases the result was understandably seldom a success. But in these few songs there is evidence of a conscious attempt at simple description. The ballads fail mainly on the dramatic level, though also because of poor or unsuitable verse. But if Schumann was a lame dramatist, he was an athletic caricaturist, as we know from his piano music, and it is no surprise to find him deploying this gift with success even on subjects not directly related—as most of his keyboard portraits were—to himself.

So it seems likely that the three Geibel songs, op. 30, all of them straightforward character-sketches in the tradition of Papageno's 'Der Vogelfänger', were written with the idea of tapping the vein of 'Die Kartenlegerin'. Once again the treatment is descriptive, the musical substance prosaic. Indeed, in the case of 'Der Page', Schumann seems so determined to maintain his objective stance that a poem which cries out for some measure of passionate involvement becomes a thoroughly bland and featureless song. However its companions, 'Der Knabe mit dem Wunderhorn' and 'Der Hidalgo', are more personable. In both, the fact that the subject is a horseman lends wings to the composer's rhythmic imagination, as does the suggestion of obvious instrumental effects—horns, guitars, mandolines. 'Der Hidalgo' rides to an ordinary bolero, but the contrasting middle section about the ladies of Seville is sufficiently roguish in manner and flowery in matter to establish the hidalgo as a larger-than-life character. The boy with his magic horn is, by comparison, lacking in temperament, perhaps because the accompaniment is too obviously a collection of effects strung together with chords. Part of the fault may also lie in the word-setting, which forces Geibel's poem to fit the rhythm much against its will. Even so the song has vivacity and a certain carefree gaiety; and in particular an evocative ending as the boy rides off into the setting sun.

The one other Geibel setting of this year, the partially experimental 'Sehnsucht', is of interest only for its curious use of a grand rhetorical piano cadenza at the beginning and end in an endeavour to create a suitably dramatic climate for the setting itself. The effect is inevitably artificial. But not all Schumann's attempts at a dramatic type of lyric are as strained as this. No less than three of the four Hans Andersen songs in op. 40 are of this type, and all three are comparatively successful—though they remain practically unknown even to singers specializing in Schumann. The composer came across the Andersen poems in German translation among Chamisso's *Gedichte*, where he also found the Greek poem which completes the collection of five songs. There is some evidence of a conscious arrangement within the set. It starts and ends in G, Nos. 2 and 3 are in D minor, while No. 4 opens ambiguously in that key before moving firmly to its close in G major. As regards subject-matter, four at least of the songs are about betrayal, whether personal or in some sense cosmic. In 'Muttertraum', the mother's blissful hopes for her child's future are set against the eventual reality of his death on the gallows; 'Der Soldat', whose meaning is ambiguous, can be interpreted as a parable about betrayed friendship; and 'Der Spielmann' goes back to the familiar image of the tragic wedding, with the added piquancy for Schumann that the discarded lover is a musician threatened by madness. As a counterbalance to this, 'Verratene Liebe' sings happily of a betrayal which nobody really minds.

The opening song, 'Märzveilchen', suggests more gently that life may not always be what it seems: its identification of beauty and promised pain—the need for mercy on the boy who falls in love—is typical of German romantic lyricism, and it is no surprise that Schumann's setting reverts to the delicate chromaticism of earlier flower-songs, 'Im wunderschönen Monat Mai' or 'Jasminenstrauch'. From the start, 'Muttertraum' is grander, even though, strictly interpreted, the voice never rises much above a *piano* dynamic. The scene is set by the betrayal music from 'Zwielicht', which both introduces the voice and runs on as accompaniment to the first two and a half verses, with stinging dissonances set up between voice and piano by the winding chromatics of the right hand and the left hand's tendency to move on the odd half-beat:

The mother's joy is thus already seen through a curtain of predestined evil. Later Schumann underlines this point by moving unexpectedly to a broad major as the ravens make the threat explicit (repeated chords as in 'Zwielicht'); the rich E flat colouring suggests fulfilment, and finality. At the end the piano winds on in D minor, a grim reminder of the endless spiral of destiny and the insignificance of the individual.

A similar type of image also dominates the third song, 'Der Soldat'. This time the music is cast as a solemn march escorting a condemned soldier to his execution. Purely from the descriptive point of view, the setting is wonderfully vivid: the soft drum-rolls, the halting rhythm of a military slow-march, and the remorseless tempo broken only at the climax, where the voice slips into hushed recitative over soft *tremolando* chords. But the effect is cold, in the way that *opera seria* can strike us as cold, sacrificing personal involvement to a more loftily generalized style of tragedy. From neither poem nor song do we sense the exact character of the ending, whether ironic, because the soldier is hit only by his friend's bullet, or in the nature of poetic justice, because his crime has somehow involved a betrayal of that friendship. The enigma is only deepened by the soft chromatic postlude, closing questioningly on a dominant chord.

'Der Spielmann' obviously recalls the Heine wedding songs, 'Das ist ein Flöten und Geigen' and the first part of 'Der arme Peter', with their ironic waltz music. Again the poet finds himself at his beloved's wedding to another man, but now he is cast, horrifyingly, as the violinist who must play the dance. Andersen envisages a music of diabolic power, the power to convert mental processes into physical ones so that the body literally disintegrates under psychological stress. At first the poet merely relates these nightmare events, but towards the end there is a moment of truth as realization dawns that he is himself their victim. Schumann's setting is stronger in the first part, where the scene is described from a distance, than in the second, where the experience becomes personal. In particular, he makes brilliant use of imagined fragments of waltz music as a violin might play it, complete with double-stopping and up and down bows. But the material itself is conventional—not least for its dependence on the diminished seventh chord. And the quiet, docile ending conveys little of the anguish and despair in the poem. For once Schumann has shied away from his text.

These two songs, 'Der Spielmann' and 'Der Soldat', are extreme instances of Schumann's attempt to introduce theatre into the lied. Like 'Muttertraum', they are cast in a grander manner than such obvious parallels as 'Das ist ein Flöten und Geigen' or 'Die beiden Grenadiere', and their psychological penetration is correspondingly reduced. That they succeed at all is surprising, for Schumann had already shown that he had no great command of explicit dramatic style; and the point is underlined by the fact that both songs end inconclusively—the one with Schumann's favourite recitative device and a few dominant chords, the other with an extended and rather bland coda, where Schumann's typical self would surely have made some decisive psycho-musical gesture. In the context, the brilliance of the final song, 'Verratene Liebe', is therefore doubly telling. For this tiny comedy of betrayal, Schumann reverts to the coquettish style of 'Die Kartenlegerin', with its athletic word-setting and sparkling accompaniment. But now the whole song is over in thirty seconds. At the start all is secrecy: piano and voice confide softly in one another. Then gradually the secret gets about, and by the end both are chattering merrily to the whole town about their love. There is one irresistible moment of pure knockabout farce when the star falls upwards, by an indiscreet major ninth. The whole effect is to make light of the portentousness of the preceding songs, and more than anything it recalls the end of Beethoven's F minor Quartet, with its 'joke' coda.

If op. 40, with all its faults, is the most interesting of Schumann's unknown collections, its immediate successor, the six Reinick songs of op. 36, must be one of the dullest. As usual, the fault lies mainly with the choice of texts. Reinick's lyrics are overextended and unctuous. But where Schubert might nevertheless have turned their scene-painting to good account, Schumann was hopelessly shackled by the plodding character of the verse and hardly seems to have noticed its bright sense of location. The very first song, 'Sonntags am Rhein', is a case in point. Reinick's description of a glittering Sunday morning by the Rhine has, for all its naivety, a certain picture-book vividness in primary blues and yellows.* But Schumann, at his most earnest, could get no further than the idea of an organ playing the good people into church, so that the song has the character of a hymn, square in phrase and accompanied only by repeated chords and an imitative bass-line. At this stage of his song-writing chordal figuration is a sure sign that the composer's genius is dormant. So in the third song, 'Nichts Schöneres', the innocent beauty of the poem's underlying idea about the bliss of marital union finds no echo in Schumann's setting, though it must have found one in his heart. All that is left is the artless charm of the poetry, expressed by an unvaried

---

* Reinick was in fact a painter as well as a poet.

six-eight rhythm, insipid harmonies, and a strophic form whose plainness is barely concealed by the appearance of its second verse (of three) in the dominant.

The final song, 'Liebesbotschaft', is still more of a fall from grace, with its octave doubling of the voice (cf. 'Wehmut') and contrived alternation of themes. Eric Sams found its main theme in a song by Clara, and although no external evidence supports the conclusion one is tempted to suggest that this song, too, may be largely her work.

Not all the Reinick settings are on this level. The best-known of them, 'An dem Sonnenschein', has a genuine folk-song freshness which looks forward to the *Liederalbum für die Jugend* of nine years later. And although 'Ständchen', with its guitar-like accompaniment, is too short-winded to impress itself firmly on the memory, it has a somnolent appeal, like a song half remembered from a dream. Both pieces suffer from colourless harmony, a consistent feature of Schumann's songs between *Dichterliebe* and his wedding. Of the Reinick collection, only 'Dichters Genesung' has real harmonic interest, which it owes to the element of fantasy and magic in the poem. Yet even here, Schumann failed to create music of special vitality. As before, the repeated quaver chords are a routine rather than apt accompaniment, and only when they break down into a fluttering image of dancing elves does the song come to life—albeit in a manner indebted to Mendelssohn. But the end is contrived. The triumphant coda is not only over-hearty in itself, but pushes back the main reprise so that the music has the poet waken while the text is still describing his dream. Finally, the postlude is a rare example in Schumann of new coda material sounding as irrelevant to the rest of the song as it looks.

The Reinick songs were completed in August 1840. Perhaps by then Schumann was too preoccupied for whole-hearted composition, for on the first of that month had come the final legal consent to his marriage, and it was now only a matter of weeks before the wedding. It took place at last on 12 September at the village of Schönefeld, not far from Leipzig. No compositions are known to date from September, but there are some, once again vocal, from October and an increasing flow up to the end of the year. In these songs one naturally searches for evidence of change or renewal in Schumann's approach to his art, but in fact the evidence points the other way, to a continuation of tendencies already noted in his work since *Dichterliebe*. Once again we find an interest in narrative and dramatic writing. Its influence is felt not only in the scale of the songs but also in their vocal and instrumental style, which is bolder, and occasionally grander, than in the lyrics of phases 1 and 2. At the same time smaller, more delicate poems continue to appear. And as before, the quality of the music is very unequal, generally reflecting the quality of the verses set.

The most striking songs of this phase are the two Eichendorff settings, 'Der Schatzgräber' and 'Frühlingsfahrt', which Schumann eventually published with 'Abends am Strand' in 1844 as the *Romanzen und Balladen*, op. 45. 'Frühlingsfahrt' is of interest as an attempt to combine the 'Freisinn' type of marching-song with the narrative, dramatic elements of the ballad. The march music which serves for the first three and the last of six verses, is bright and memorable. But Schumann seems to have been puzzled how to render the darker central verses without losing rhythmic impetus, and his solution—to develop the march material while slowing down the tempo—is a compromise which serves neither purpose. 'Der Schatzgräber', though a genuine ballad, is closer in style to the dramatic tableaux of op. 40, and like them makes its effect rather by evocation of atmosphere than by close personal identification with a central character. In the heaving chromatic figure of the prelude Schumann found a perfect musical evocation of effortful and illicit digging, while later on the piano has a spine-chilling outburst of manic laughter as the mine caves in on the unfortunate prospector. But the significance of 'Der Schatzgräber' lies above all in its unique (for Schumann) synthesis between dramatic and musical form. Where most of his ballads offer little more than a slavish reproduction in music of a verse narrative, this compact work comes much closer to a musico-dramatic type of design in which the whole flavour and force of the poem is distilled into musical material and then re-formed along musical lines. It is a technique much in evidence in Schumann's lyric miniatures, where feeling—rather than action—is involved. But it seldom appears in dramatic contexts.

Certainly it is absent from the contemporary 'Blondels Lied', a setting of a ballad by the poet of Schubert's 'Taubenpost', Johann Seidl. The work is an example of a salon ballad, a narrative entertainment rendered more sociable by music but with music always the servant of declamation. Perhaps the story would be sung by one person while the rest joined in for the refrain, 'Suche treu, so findest du!', whose musical function is that of the chorus in 'Die rote Hanne'. Not for the first time in his ballads, Schumann tries to manufacture excitement by a gradual *accelerando*; but the music, with its unvaried crotchet rhythms and block chords, vigorously resists the attempt.

If Schumann showed doubtful taste in setting such verse, his choice of lyric poets at this period is scarcely more distinguished. Heine, Eichendorff and Chamisso are now replaced by Georg Zimmermann, Abraham Fröhlich, (probably) Lily Bernhard, a friend of Clara's, and Justinus Kerner, the poet of Schumann's earliest efforts at song-writing. 'Nur ein lächelnder Blick', to a poem by Zimmermann, has the distinction of being perhaps the most derided song of any by the great lieder composers. Yet one feels that if 'Die Nonne' or 'Mädchen-Schwermut' were as known they would be as detested, for all three share that cloying vein of chromatic harmony so favoured by the mid nineteenth century to express fashionable minor ailments of the heart, and normally so uncharacteristic of Schumann. Of the three, indeed, 'Nur ein lächelnder Blick' is the most accomplished, though the closing bars of 'Die Nonne', with their almost Wagnerian harmonic colouring and unresolved final dominant seventh, have a certain curiosity value apart from the intrinsic quality of the song:

The Kerner songs are another matter, as we might expect from their number, for altogether fourteen were composed during November and December of this year. For many years a doctor in the Swabian town of Weinsberg, Kerner was known for his investigations into psychic disturbance, as well as for his poetry, which shows traces of mysticism over and above the routine symbolism of German romantic verse. Schumann apparently chose more or less at random. His settings include conventional lyrics of a pessimistic cast, alongside veiled epigrams such as 'Wer machte dich so krank?', bold drinking and marching-songs of an aspiring nature, and even one near-ballad. Even the songs finally included in the *Zwölf Gedichte*, op. 35, have no perceptible pattern, and vary considerably in both scale and manner, though we have the evidence of a sometimes laboriously coherent key sequence to show that the composer intended some higher unity beyond the superficial contrasts.*

The effect on Schumann's lyrical writing of his recent ventures into a more dramatic style is to make it bolder and more muscular, sometimes to the point of grandiloquence, especially when the verse itself has lofty pretensions. Thus few of the Kerner songs evince that subtle feeling of things unsaid which is such a feature of the Heine and Eichendorff songs. One has only to compare the first Kerner setting, 'Lust

---

* A good instance is 'Stirb, Lieb' und Freud'!', which starts in A flat but ends in the dominant of F minor, after which the following song, 'Wanderlust', announces itself with a ceremonial unison F, the dominant of its own key, B flat. Apart from a superficial resemblance in the idea of parting or separation, there is no other connection between either the songs or their poems.

der Sturmnacht', with the passingly similar 'Schöne Fremde' from op. 39, to see how explicit statement has replaced implied suggestion. Another interesting result is that the piano postlude, though still important, no longer illuminates new facets of poem or music, but now fulfils the more prosaic function of anticlimax, usually around material already heard. Even the accompaniments lack their former diversity. Occasionally, as at a famous point in 'Auf das Trinkglas eines verstorbenen Freundes', Schumann's special genius for the keyboard shows itself. But as often the piano writing is conventional and subordinate, with interest concentrated on the voice.

Thus the turbulent syncopations of 'Lust der Sturmnacht' throw off no counter-melody, unlike those of 'Schöne Fremde'. Nor, for all their vigour, do they convey the terror, as opposed to the sheer force, of a stormy night. Instead the emphasis is on the 'indoor' feeling of Kerner's poem, where the storm is relished from behind rattling window-panes with a roaring fire in the hearth and a hot-water bottle (apparently human) in the bed. However, within its limits the song has fine variety. The apparently inflexible accompaniment figure adapts itself well to the poem's central idea of the inner tranquillity created by love, and there is a grandly defiant ending (founded on a reprise of the opening music) which only a composer with a strong instinct for underlying ideas in poetry would have considered as a setting of Kerner's 'mich umfängt des Himmels Helle' ('heaven's radiance encircles me').

Yet Schumann's instincts occasionally let him down, and nowhere more than in 'Stille Tränen', later in this Kerner cycle. The poem is bitter and pessimistic: even the bright things of life are no more than a façade concealing sorrow and pain. But for Schumann the crucial verse is the first, where the poet moves in wonder beneath the blue vault of the sky, and his setting is in the nature of an apotheosis, a hymn to the ultimate beauty of existence. The result, if perverse, is certainly impressive. The song is dominated by repeated piano chords rather in the manner of 'Die Lotosblume', and a broadly phrased vocal melody which carries the voice up to a heroic top B flat on, of all things, the word 'Schmerz' ('grief'). But the music itself conveys anything but a sense of pain. After the voice has finished (at 'stets fröhlich sei sein Herz') Schumann makes a long repeat of the main theme for piano solo, a passage much indebted to Chopin, ending with yet another ecstatic phrase for the voice and an extended postlude in which the music at last calms down into some semblance of the poem's ambiguity.

The strange thing about 'Stille Tränen' is that although the music clearly springs from a spontaneous reaction to a line or two of the poem—rather than its whole meaning—Schumann nevertheless saw some larger allegorical significance in his setting. This is apparent from the fact that he preceded and followed it with a group of minute songs which are virtually meaningless except in relation to the larger song. 'Frage' has the (unnecessary) technical function of bridging the keychange from the E flat of 'Stille Liebe' to the C major of 'Stille Tränen'. But the 'question' of its title is obviously meant to be significant, as though 'Stille Tränen' were to supply the answer. The cycle ends with two poems, 'Wer machte dich so krank?' and 'Alte Laute', spatchcocked into one strophic song in the character of an envoi—a visionary farewell to the pain and exhaustion of this world and hopefully a glimpse into the next. The feeling here is very much that of an epilogue, and it is hard to imagine the song making much effect out of context. Yet an examination of the four poems, 'Frage', 'Stille Tränen', and these last two, reveals no clear thread of meaning, except perhaps the idea of nature consoling human grief, and this is in any case contradicted by the final poem, 'Alte Laute', where even the flowers and birdsong have lost their power to heal.

The earlier songs in the collection enjoy a more independent existence, and their cut is generally more conventional than that of 'Stille Tränen'. 'Wanderlust', yet another marching-song after 'Freisinn', is too long for its plain, hearty melody, a fault which Schumann aggravates by reprising the tune (for the third time) to a repeat of the poet's first verse. In between is a more ingratiating section about the familiar comforts to be had in foreign parts, couched in Schumann's favourite flattened submediant (cf. 'Ich wandelte unter den Bäumen'). The traveller in 'Wanderung', like his counterpart in 'Der Knabe mit dem Wunderhorn', goes on horseback, so his journey is sooner ended. But here, too, there is a certain harmonic drabness (masquerading as bluff simplicity), and a monotony of rhythm only partly mitigated by the prancing figuration of the accompaniment. Schumann's other, more successful, outdoor manner, the yearning, elegiac vein of the Burns settings in *Myrten* or such Heine lyrics as 'Hör ich das Liedchen klingen', is also represented in op. 35. 'Erstes Grün' in particular recalls the Burns songs of parting and separation, with its sorrowful opening minor triad and sweet melancholy tune, treated strophically. That Schumann is happier in this mood is left beyond doubt by the comparative subtlety of the piano writing, both in accompaniment and in the delicate interlude music, with its wistful opposition of G major to the G minor of the song. The companion to 'Erstes Grün' is 'Sehnsucht nach der Waldgegend', also in G minor. This beautiful song of yearning for the woodlands (of *Liederkreis*?) uses its main theme more sparingly; in fact it is heard just twice, at the start and the finish. The middle section develops a warm counter-melody in F over piano figuration descriptive of the joys of forest life. An unusual feature of the song is its irregular rhythm- and phrase-structure. In verses 1 and 5 the first two lines have two bars of music each followed by two lines with a bar each; the middle three verses are more regular, but with more complex accompaniment rhythms. Such asymmetries are often to be found in Schumann's more deeply felt songs, and it may be that their absence from a later song of op. 35, 'Stille Liebe', accounts for the comparative inertia of this piece. 'Stille Liebe' is possibly the nearest approach among the Kerner songs to the technical character of *Dichterliebe* and indeed its poignantly sensitive piano part would not be out of place in that cycle. But the *Dichterliebe* Schumann would have found a better melody for a better poem—or, having chosen a simple, folkish tune, would surely have harmonized it with greater piquancy and inward suggestion.

If plain harmony is a fault in 'Stille Liebe', it is a virtue, or at least a valid effect, in the two remaining songs, 'Stirb, Lieb' und Freud'!' and 'Auf das Trinkglas eines verstorbenen Freundes'. For these otherwise contrasted works, Schumann reverts to the somewhat hymnic, narrative style of 'Die rote Hanne'. But no longer is the music subservient to the text: on the contrary the musical description is now so important that Schumann even consciously allows it to override the emotional content of the poetry. This is true, at least, of 'Stirb, Lieb' und Freud'!', where the solemn processional music accompanies the heroine through all her genuflections, and only stops, with her, at the high altar, leaving Schumann uncharacteristically baffled how to render the more personal closing lines, which are the whole emotional point of the poem. This song, incidentally, was plainly influenced by Bach, whose music Schumann and Mendelssohn had worked hard to reintroduce to German audiences: that it also anticipates Brahms, who was himself influenced by the German baroque, is not really surprising. Although 'Auf das Trinkglas eines verstorbenen Freundes' displays neither of these similarities, it does share the richly diatonic harmony and almost ceremonial grandeur of 'Stirb, Lieb' und Freud'!' But this time, with no narrative to distract him, Schumann is more attentive to the mystical quality of Kerner's poem, and the result is a song of real and unexpected vision. The solemnity of the opening, with its plain E flat harmonies and awkward feminine endings, is perhaps deliberately empty and conventional. However, at the words 'Jetzt sollst du mir gefüllet sein', the music, like the dead friend's glass, suddenly fills with new meaning. The key darkens magically to D flat, and there follows a mysterious passage in which the idea of a secret bond between the living and the dead is matched by other-worldly chromatics of almost Schubertian power. The second verse (actually the poem's fourth) starts like the first. But then, as the setting moon takes with it the last echoes of friendship, Schumann finds an unforgettable image for the shimmering moonlight: soft repeated piano chords suspended in harmonic space, and a radiant vocal line:

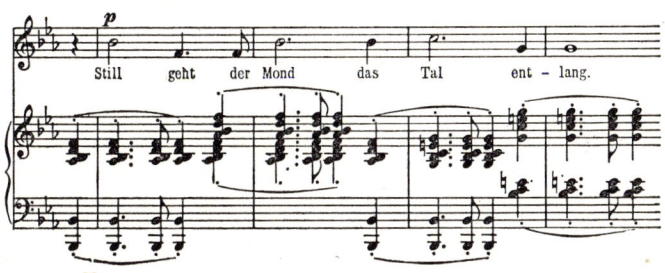

The image is both realistic and visionary, and even a comparatively dull postlude fails to diminish its power.

Two other Kerner settings were made at this period, with the coincidentally similar titles 'Sängers Trost' and 'Trost im Gesang'. Both are negligible, and both were omitted from op. 35 when it was published in July 1841. 'Sängers Trost', a distant relative of 'Nur ein lächelnder Blick', is notable mainly for the tonal ambiguity of its start (G minor for a song in B flat) and for the high *tessitura* of the vocal line, which ranges entirely between written A above middle C and the A flat above. 'Trost im Gesang', possibly the earliest of the Kerner songs, still has 'Die rote Hanne' on the brain, its absolute squareness of phrase merely emphasized by the final-line repeats in each verse.

That Schumann should have written such poor songs in 1840 is less surprising than that their number should have been so few. They are nothing more than the occasional and inevitable failures which confront all great artists, and particularly those who exercise their self-critical faculty after, rather than during, the creative process. On the whole we can say that Schumann ended this extraordinary year of song in worthy fashion, with fine works like 'Sehnsucht nach der Waldgegend' and 'Auf das Trinkglas eines verstorbenen Freundes'. Yet it cannot be denied that in the later months the completely successful song is less common than before, and there is evidence that the flame which burnt so brightly before the wedding is now often no more than a comfortable glow, flaming up with passing draughts of inspiration but as a rule only too well insulated against them. Christmas 1840 seems finally to have quenched the flame. Schumann was now increasingly interested in writing symphonies, and the few songs composed in the New Year are trivial and uncharacteristic, clearly the work of a preoccupied mind. Indeed if we are to accept the official attributions, some of the most finished music in them is actually by Clara.

The *Zwölf Gedichte*, op. 37, include at least three songs by her, and internal evidence suggests that her contribution may not have ended there. In the first song, 'Der Himmel hat eine Träne geweint', for instance, the opening bars of each verse and the postlude are clearly Schumann's work (cf. 'Widmung') while the remainder is in quite a different style. The songs acknowledged to be by Clara show the influence of Mendelssohn (especially in the piano writing) rather than Schumann, and their charm, though real, now seems bland and complacent. Elsewhere in the cycle where Mendelssohn seems to be hovering overhead, one may again suspect a touch of wifely collaboration.

The poems are from Rückert's *Liebesfrühling*, but more in the facile vein of 'Zum Schluss' than the passionate one of 'Widmung'. The English word which best describes them is 'sentimental', and in this they match Schumann's conception of the cycle as a perfect artistic expression of his and Clara's perfect marital empathy. Such an idea now strikes us as touching rather than stimulating, but we should remember that the Schumanns lived in an age of social duetting, which saw agreeable communal art as the symptom of a healthy culture. Sure enough, op. 37 includes two duets (one of them canonic), and a third, solo song—'Liebste, was kann denn uns scheiden?'—probably designed to be sung by two voices in unison or alternation, with a bar or two of close harmony at the end of each verse. Musically they are no better and no worse than many of Schumann's vocal ensembles, a genre in which his writing was almost invariably cramped and simplistic. Of the genuine solo songs, the most successful, perhaps surprisingly, are the two longest, 'Flügel! Flügel!' and 'Rose, Meer und Sonne'. The first of these contains much that is pedestrian, and some memorable moments of which the loftiest, in every sense, is the soaring F sharp minor cadence on the word 'Sternentor'. The accompaniment, interestingly, is almost orchestral in character. 'Rose, Meer und Sonne', a typical attempt to adopt nature as a paradigm of human feeling, suffers from too many repeats of its admittedly attractive melody, a fault which Schumann compounds by carrying the tune over, in a much less agreeable form, into the next song, 'O Sonn', o Meer, o Rose!' The interest of both is that their postlude (much shortened in the second song) clearly refers back to the end of *Dichterliebe*, though its failure to recapture the spirit, as opposed to the notes, of that work is not wholly unexpected. Little need be said of the remaining songs, 'O ihr Herren' and 'Ich hab' in mich gesogen', which embalm obsequious verses in properly ingratiating music. The latter must qualify as one of Schumann's feeblest songs, with its interminably slithering accompaniment and short-winded vocal phrases, unbroken by any variation in texture.

With the Rückert cycle, Schumann's first great spell of song-writing is at an end. Between January 1841 and 1847 he composed only two or three insignificant songs, and possibly not even these, for all are of uncertain date. Christern's 'Ich wand're nicht', for instance, is dated December 1841, but its style is closely akin to that of 'Nichts Schöneres' and some of the other Reinick songs, so it may well have been composed before the wedding. The sonorous but uninventive 'Auf dem Rhein' also has the smack of late 1840, a period of many chordal accompaniments, though the date usually given is 1846. Of greater intrinsic value is the setting of Heine's three-part poem 'Tragödie', for which the earliest known date is November 1841, in a version for chorus and orchestra. There is some support for Eric Sams's postulation of an 1840 original for this work, possibly even in the definitive version for voice and piano. The first song, 'Entflieh' mit mir', is strongly reminiscent of 'Er, der Herrlichste von allen', both in harmony and rhythm, and in its excited use of the turn. The other two songs, on the other hand, suggest a slightly later style. 'Es fiel ein Reif' is a hesitant folk-song imitation in the manner of 'Mädchen-Schwermut', while its companion calls to mind the square little duet which concludes the Rückert cycle, op. 37, though Heine's more pointed lyric draws a sharper musical response, especially in its elegiac postlude. If 'Tragödie' were in fact composed in late 1840 or early 1841, it would make an apt end to a year dominated by settings of Heine, not least because after that year Schumann never again set words by this poet.

5   *Symphonic Interlude*

'My highest wish is that he should compose for orchestra—that is his field! May I succeed in bringing him to it.' To many, if not most, composers of Schumann's day the greatest art was to be sought in the greatest dimensions: in piano music the sonata; but for preference in all music the symphony, the cantata and the opera. As a reviewer, Schumann is often to be found urging his contemporaries to stop wasting their talents on small-scale composition and to turn instead to the 'higher' symphonic forms. And even before 1841 his own finest piano and vocal works tend towards a synthesis of the self-contained miniature into a grand, integrated design, though the process is generally either subconscious or (as with *Myrten*) post-rationalized. Clara's wifely amibitions for him were thus an echo of his own, and their fulfilment only a matter of time. In fact Schumann probably never regarded song-writing as anything but an interim phase between composing for the piano and for its natural extension, the orchestra. Once serious orchestral and choral writing was under way, song would inevitably lose its attraction.

After tentative experiments in the autumn, this happened at last in late January 1841. As with the songs a year before, the music came swiftly once Schumann's inhibitions had been removed, and the B flat Symphony was composed in short score in the space of only four days. By September he had also completed the *Overture, Scherzo and Finale*, op. 52, the A minor Fantasy (later the first movement of the Piano Concerto), the original version of the D minor Symphony and a full-blown sketch for a third symphony in C minor, subsequently discarded. This outburst of symphonic writing was to be a prelude to still more recondite schemes. The next year, 1842, for instance, was productive mainly of chamber music: all three of the op. 41 string quartets, the piano quintet and quartet. And in 1843 came the work which, above all, Schumann regarded as his most important to date, the oratorio *Paradise and the Peri*. Individually and as a whole, these scores carried him beyond anything he had written previously, for, quite apart from their scale, they included his first fully mature attempts at composition without piano. True, the 1840 songs had accustomed him to writing for a medium other than his own: but the addition of a single line to a piano piece (which is in effect how many of the early songs were formed) hardly meant a radical change in the underlying instrumental approach compared with that involved in working with an orchestra or string quartet. Thus the music of this period has to support a double burden. Not only is it naturally more intellectual than most of Schumann's previous work, but it is also more abstract in character as a result of the loss of the close contact with his medium that he had always enjoyed when writing piano music. At first the burden is carried lightly enough. There are few more spontaneous works than the B flat Symphony or the A minor concerto movement. But in 1843 there is evidence, both internal and external, that composition is no longer the simple process of self-expression it was three or four years before. In most of the works written after that date including more than a hundred songs (but with the single exception of the E flat Symphony), even the finest music has a quality of straining for something not immediately, and hardly to be brought, within reach.

The mental strain, as always with Schumann, provoked nervous symptoms. In August 1844, after accompanying Clara on a difficult four-month concert tour of Russia, he suffered a breakdown which proved so serious that the couple finally (in December) decided to settle in Dresden, where musical life was generally more easy-going than in Leipzig. The next two years were a time of rehabilitation. They saw the composition of the C major Symphony, and the completion of the Piano Concerto, but little other important creative work, and much of 1845 was spent in renewing acquaintance with Bach, in the composition of fugues and canons for piano, organ and pedal-piano, and in contrapuntal studies with Clara. In Dresden Schumann met Wagner, who was *Kapellmeister* at the opera, for the first time, and attended an early performance of *Tannhäuser* (in November 1845). Meanwhile his own search for an opera text continued. He had already, in 1844, composed some of what later became the third part of *Scenes from Goethe's 'Faust'*, intending it to form part of an opera on the subject; he had toyed with Byron's *The Corsair*, Hoffmann's *Doge und Dogaressa*, and, according to Wasielewski, upwards of twenty other subjects, before finally settling, in 1847, on Hebbel's *Genoveva*. Thus by the time he returned seriously to song-writing, in 1849, the whole ethos of his work had changed. From being a miniaturist and character-artist with a wide reputation as critic and editor, he was transformed into a symphonist, an opera-composer (*Genoveva* was completed in 1848 though not staged until 1850), and a choralist in every field from the dramatic cantata down through the choral lied with orchestra to the part-song and vocal ensemble. It is hardly surprising that most of the songs of 1849, varied as they are, should share at least the one superficial quality of having little or nothing in common with the 1840 lyrics.

During the first four years in Dresden Schumann composed only three songs, including the tiny 'Soldatenlied', which was published in a book of children's songs in 1845 and probably written about the time of the move. Its sole interest is that it foreshadows a whole group of settings to the same poet, Hoffmann von Fallersleben, which Schumann made four years later in his *Liederalbum für die Jugend*. The other two songs, both composed in 1847, are of much greater significance, if only because they are Schumann's first settings of one of the finest lyric poets of his day, Eduard Mörike. It seems curious that the 1840 songs include none by Mörike, who was six years Schumann's senior and had already published many of his best poems; but less strange that these two songs were not the prelude to a whole collection, since Schumann was by then considerably less attracted than before by the concise or suggestive short lyric. The first setting, 'Die Soldatenbraut', is a bright marching song in the now familiar idiom and key (B flat), but with the added charm that its 'hero' is a girl, of both resource and good humour. One can almost sense Schumann looking out his existing songs to remind himself of old habits: the drum-roll of 'Der Soldat', the march rhythm, arpeggios and dactyllic middle section of 'Wanderlust', the song-form completed by a repeat of the poet's first verse, and the subdominant harmonies of the postlude. Indeed 'Die Soldatenbraut' is so like the later songs of 1840 that its companion, 'Das verlassene Mägdelein', comes as a surprise, for here we discover quite a new Schumann. True, the melody (which is complete in the piano rather than the voice) bears a superficial resemblance to the gloomy folk-song themes of 'Mädchen-Schwermut' and 'Es fiel ein Reif' from 'Tragödie'; true also that the intensity and economy of the writing hark back to *Dichterliebe*. But in reality manner and matter are alike novel. Gone is the simple tune rendered articulate by an isolated chromatic interval or dissonant harmony. In its place is a melodic strand whose whole motion is chromatic, interwoven with two such strands to make a light but close-knit fabric of dissonance—a cloak of misery for the forsaken girl. Clearly the influence of Bach is at work, but as yet incompletely assimilated, as though Schumann still had in mind his intensive contrapuntal studies of two years before.* Not surprisingly the song seems to have cost him some effort, and while its design is meticulously organic it lacks the rightness and apparent spontaneity of such a carefully built song as 'Das ist ein Flöten und Geigen'. The agonizing precision of Mörike's poem has somehow become a generalized image of sorrow, touching rather than profoundly disturbing.

Schumann wrote no songs in 1848, the year of the Paris revolution and disturbances in Berlin (with which he was theoretically, rather than actively, in sympathy). The following year, however, marks a serious return to song-writing. From 1849 date the whole of the *Liederalbum für die Jugend*, the *Wilhelm Meister* songs, op. 98, and the Byron songs, op. 95; and this is also the year of three important collections of vocal ensembles, the *Spanisches Liederspiel*, op. 74, and *Spanisches Liebeslieder*, op. 138, to poems translated by Geibel, and the *Minnespiel*, op. 101, from Rückert's *Liebesfrühling*, all of which include songs for solo voice among their duets and quartets.

The Spanish poems seem to have attracted Schumann as much as anything for their dramatic qualities, a reflection of that typically theatrical side of Spanish life which has always been so fascinating to northern Europeans. This had also been

---

* Significantly, 1847 was also the year of the seven part-songs, op. 65, which are a collection of canons for male voices.

the appeal of the much-travelled Geibel in 1840. His poems were colourful, eventful and grand, and fit to be clothed in music that was itself tending more and more to assume some of the public characteristics of music theatre. In the Spanish songs these qualities are still more pronounced, and it is easy to see why Schumann decided to call the first set *Liederspiel*, or vaudeville, even though the ensembles are not dramatic, but sociable, in their musical lay-out. One has only to examine the duets 'Erste Begegnung' or 'Liebesgram' or the curiously Purcellian soprano solo 'Melancholie' to see that in response to vivid poetry Schumann was able to direct recent baroque influences into a channel altogether appropriate to the florid and aristocratic world of the *duende*. Yet these songs retain an unmistakable leavening of German *Innigkeit*. Two other duets, 'Und schläfst du, mein Mädchen' and the gloriously sustained 'In der Nacht', could well be by Brahms, while the tenor solo 'Geständnis', is not so far in mood from a heartfelt lyric such as 'Intermezzo', though its ternary form is more mechanical and its harmonies (apart from the unusually rich piano chords— dominant seventh over a tonic pedal—with which it begins and ends) generally more stereotyped. As an afterthought, Schumann appended an operatic comic song for baritone, 'Der Contrabandiste', to this collection. It was a strange idea, and it fails, as so much German musical humour fails, for lack of true wit, notably in the piano part. But taken as a whole op. 74 is musically his most interesting and agreeable work for vocal ensemble, and one of the few which merit revival.

The later Geibel set, op. 138, differs from Schumann's other vocal works in that its accompaniment is for piano duet, though in the five solo songs, at least, there seems no compelling musical reason for this. Only 'Flutenreicher Ebro', with its left-hand guitar imitations and brightly ornamented primo chords, could not be reduced for one piano without significant loss. In the other songs the upper part is largely ornamental. In 'Weh, wie zornig' it imitates the tenor voice as if in mockery of the petulant girl sulking on the hillside. But in 'Tief im Herzen', a heavy soprano lament accompanied by thick harp chords in the lower part, the primo is almost embarrassingly short of material, and merely interpolates tiny phrases before each voice entry as if to keep itself occupied. The two best songs are undoubtedly those which distribute a lightweight accompaniment equally, though in neither case would it require a Liszt to play the essential notes with two hands. 'Hoch, hoch sind die Berge' is a strange song to find in a Spanish *Liederbuch*, for it most closely resembles Schumann's Burns settings, as though the idea of a forsaken lover in the highlands intuitively transported him to the country of 'Im Westen'. But if it lacks the special poignancy of those earlier songs, there is real charm in the flowing quavers of its accompaniment and the shapely vocal melody. The other tenor song, 'O wie lieblich ist das Mädchen', is a wholly enchanting example of the *Gesang* style, strophic in design and popular in conception, but with deceptive subtlety of rhythm and phrase-length. As so often in Schumann, a leaning towards the subdominant lends warmth and a faint sense of indulgence.

Charming and varied though they are, these Geibel collections are typical of Schumann neither in his early lyric style nor in his later, more melodramatic one. They are a diversion, entertaining but peripheral. The same cannot be said of the *Minnespiel*, op. 101, which clearly represents an attempt to recapture the mood of earlier Rückert settings, including op. 37, of which Schumann presumably still thought highly (indeed one of the quartets is a new setting of 'Schön ist das Fest des Lenzes', which appears as a duet in the 1841 collection). The older, less spontaneous Schumann wrote comparatively seldom in the simple lyric vein, and the delicate but precious Rückert was hardly the poet to help him recapture its more piquant musical qualities. One wonders what he would have made of Heine; but significantly no Heine was set. Instead we have these unwieldy love-songs, a strange and unhappy compromise between old influences and new. Officially there are four of them, but one could say that there are five, since the first, 'Meine Töne still und heiter' (for tenor), is in every sense double: a setting of two poems to two tunes in two keys, almost like an aria with its cabaletta. The strophic, and therefore repetitive, form of the second part endeavours to bulldoze the listener into accepting C major as the home key, but it is the emotionally more elusive first part which catches the imagination, and the ear remains puzzled by the apparently unmotivated change.

Possibly Schumann wanted the first two complete songs to be heard as a pair, since the second, 'Liebster, deine Worte stehlen' (for soprano), starts on a chord of C major but modulates at once, via a short recitative, back into G major and the effusive mood of part 1 of 'Meine Töne'. It must be said, however, that the music of neither piece is strong enough to support such an edifice. Altogether more interesting are the two remaining solos, both of which show the new influence of Bach, and particularly of his accompanied recitatives, where a slow, even melody so often rides above a more restless accompaniment which probes, like a dentist's drill, into its most painful harmonic roots. Schumann's 'O Freund, mein Schirm, mein Schutz' is generally agreed to be too tortured for its own good: its relentless accented passing notes smack too much of self-pity. But the comparatively optimistic 'Mein schöner Stern' is more successful, partly perhaps because it depends on a strong vocal line to which the harmonies are subsidiary. Curiously enough its repeated piano chords, often making two or even three harmonies per bar, recall those of 'Er, der Herrlichste von allen', as does the slower-striding bass. In spirit the two songs could hardly be less similar.

Before we pass on to the main solo song collections of the Dresden period, something should be said here about the *Liederalbum für die Jugend*, which Schumann composed as a companion for his piano album of the previous year in April and May 1849. A number of these children's songs were written literally in the midst of Dresden's spring rising, and it may be significant that among the poems chosen by the moderately left-wing Schumann are several by Hoffmann von Fallersleben and one by J. L. Uhland, both well-known radical figures in contemporary German literature. But too much should not be made of this. Having made his choice out of instinctive sympathy, Schumann tended to ignore the social undertones of the verses, and even such an overt jibe at political bad faith as Hoffmann's 'Vom Schlaraffenland' would be treated to a setting devoid of all guile (though with plenty of musical interest as an examination of its unequal phrase structure reveals). In fact, the nine Hoffmann songs, out of twenty-four for solo voice, include most of the simplest and most genuinely childlike in the whole collection.

As his op. 68 piano pieces had shown, Schumann was gifted, if less gifted than Brahms, at compsoing simple but worthwhile music for children, without lapsing into patronage or mawkish sentimentality. Though it would be wrong to expect such pieces as 'Schmetterling' or 'Käuzlein' to contribute to an understanding of his adult music, it would equally be churlish to deny them a plain, unaffected grace, quite lacking in facile prettiness, even amid the inevitable harping on spring and shepherds' pipes. In rather a different category are the handful of songs which have claimed immortality on pure musical merit. They include the final piece, 'Kennst du das Land?' (which will be discussed below with the other songs from Goethe's *Wilhelm Meister*), if not the other two Goethe settings, the over-portentous 'Lied Lynceus des Türmers', and the attractive cautionary ballad, 'Die wandelnde Glock', which properly belongs with the simple chorus songs in the group. Once again the Mörike setting, 'Er ist's', has rarity value, though its already insubstantial charm is seriously diluted by the amorphous treatment of the poem, which leaves out words and repeats the last two lines, in whole or part, no less than eleven times to accommodate a reprise and coda. In fact a better song in this style is the Rückert 'Schneeglöckchen', which contents itself with a strophic format more in keeping with the delicate imagery of snowdrops and spring blossom.

Also of rarity value are the two songs from Schiller's *Wilhelm Tell*, 'Des Sennen Abschied' and 'Des Buben Schützenlied', though the latter, yet another marching-song in B flat, is of scant musical interest and indeed in its word-setting borders on the inept. 'Des Sennen Abschied', by contrast, is one of the most vivid of the children's songs, with its lilting *ranz des vaches* and colourful use of such imagery as the cutting off at the word 'lieblichen' (before 'Mai') to bring the cowherd back from his dreams of next spring to the nostalgia of this autumn:

The other well-known songs all deserve their fame: 'Sonntag', with its smilingly *gemütlich* tune; 'Der Sandmann', with its busy, tip-toe accompaniment; the first 'Zigeunerliedchen', a rare moment of bitterness and anguish; and especially 'Marienwürmchen', a wholly enchanting nursery-rhyme which quotes (no doubt unconsciously) from the intermezzo of the Piano Concerto.

The inclusion of Mignon's 'Kennst du das Land?' in a book of songs for (rather than about) children clearly betokened some deeper motion of the spirit than a simple desire to cover the whole spectrum of childish experience, and it is no surprise to find Schumann within a few weeks—that is, in June and July 1849—engaged in setting Mignon's other songs, along with the Harper's songs and Philine's 'Singet nicht in Trauertönen', from the novel *Wilhelm Meisters Lehrjahre*. Goethe was already much in his mind. The *Scenes from Faust* were not completed until 1850 (the overture eventually following in 1853), and it was clearly the melodramatic aspects of *Wilhelm Meister*, the tragedy of the supposed orphan Mignon and the guilt-ridden Harper, her father by his own sister, which caught the composer's imagination. His settings are above all operatic in style. They recall many aspects of the almost Wagnerian harmonic texture of *Genoveva* and *Faust*, coupled with the new symphonic type of treatment which had made those works technically possible. The accompaniments, for the first time in Schumann, are quasi-orchestral rather than pianistic, with the harp idea naturally prominent in the Harper's songs, while the whole melodic approach is that of a composer who, having composed symphonies and operas, now thinks inevitably in terms of unity by contrast, rather than identity, of themes. The concept is an ambitious one, and in particular poses serious problems of scale and proportion, for Goethe's poems—for all their charged emotional content—are still lyrics, brief in duration and leaving much unsaid. On several occasions Schumann found that a poem was too short to accommodate the music he wanted to write, and was forced either to lengthen it by the old technique of repetition, or more often to curtail his own ideas in a manner essentially foreign to their expansive theatrical nature. As a result there is a persistent sense of embarking on an important journey but missing the only train.

Ironically the only songs which could be argued to be complete successes in this respect are the foundation-stone of the cycle, 'Kennst du das Land?', which for the longest lyric nevertheless retains something of the strophic simplicity of the *Liederalbum*, and 'Singet nicht in Trauertönen', which is basically light in character. The other songs are all at least conditional failures, the condition being that they contain some of the most powerful and unforgettable music Schumann had written since the Second Symphony.

'Kennst du das Land?' was one of the most set of all German poems in the nineteenth century. Wolf's frenziedly grandiloquent version and the more straightforward settings by Beethoven and Schubert are all better known than Schumann's, yet it is Schumann's song which perhaps most nearly captures that blend of adult passion and childish bewilderment which lie at the heart of Goethe's great lyric. The setting of the words shows Schumann at his best. The simple question ingenuously posed at the start of each verse, the mounting excitement as the child's memory begins to play on her emotions, the disappointed fading out of each vision as she realizes that her dream of returning home will never be fulfilled—all these are vividly and beautifully evoked. What is perhaps denied by the strophic form is any increase of tension from verse to verse of the poem, as Mignon's mind's eye switches from the countryside of her Italian homeland to the horrors of the mountain pass which divides her from it. Schumann must have recognized this weakness from experience performing the song, for when it was republished as op. 98a, no. 1, he added the direction: 'the last two verses with increased expression'. Yet even without this artificial aid, there is room for varied characterization. The harmonies are chromatically richer than in any previous Schumann song, with much use of augmented and diminished intervals, chords of the dominant minor ninth and diminished seventh, augmented triads, and suspended dissonances of various kinds. And after all the symmetry is the poet's, not the composer's, a point seemingly ignored by Frank Walker in his somewhat tortuous defence of Wolf's setting.*

---

* *Hugo Wolf: a Biography*, revised edition (Dent, 1968), p. 248. No general criticism is of course intended of this incomparable study of Wolf's life and works.

Mignon's three other songs are given straight-through settings, but only one of them, 'Heiss' mich nicht reden', can compare for subtlety with 'Kennst du das Land?' A feature of this song is its astonishing wealth of inspiration, every detail of the poem being matched, and occasionally enhanced, by a distinctive musical idea—as at the start where after peremptory piano chords a mysterious hush falls on the word 'schweigen':

Scarcely less remarkable is the dramatic use of harmony. In the opening, 'schweigen' is on A flat after a C minor introduction; later at the word 'Gott' the music darkens to E flat minor via a German sixth (cf. the start of 'Am leuchtenden Sommermorgen'), followed by a three-word repeat which culminates in an extraordinary piano interlude with tritonal horn-calls, a huge climactic dissonance and a dispirited repeat of the poem's opening and closing lines. Not surprisingly, Schumann was unable to sustain invention of this quality. 'So lasst mich scheinen', the last song in this collection, is a disorganized piece which suffers from its failure to discover pointed accompaniment material after the halting introduction figure has vanished at bar 5. 'Nur wer die Sehnsucht kennt', on the other hand, is the victim of an almost unsettable poem whose extreme compression the new operatic Schumann could only attempt to counter by repeating the text virtually whole.

Apart from the tidy but uninspired 'Singet nicht in Trauertönen', which serves mainly for light relief, there remain the four Harper's songs. Like Mignon's they are of very unequal quality. At their best, as in 'Wer sich der Einsamkeit ergibt', they share the inventive qualities of 'Heiss' mich nicht reden', and also in rather greater measure its prolixity of material. But all four are damaged by Schumann's inability to resist harp figuration by way of accompaniment. In 'Wer nie sein Brod mit Tränen ass' the harp suddenly and inexplicably strikes up at 'Ihr führt ins Leben uns hinein' with extravagant arpeggios which dissipate the brooding, introspective gloom of the start. In 'An die Türen will ich schleichen' the harp is much less obtrusive, though it may have been its influence which led Schumann to switch suddenly to plain chords at the beginning of verse 2, thus breaking the momentum impressively created by the heavy, measured tread of the first verse. 'Wer sich der Einsamkeit ergibt' is remarkable for its use of the device which had ended 'Muttertraum', where the sudden interpolation of broad major harmonies suggested the idea of predestined fulfilment in death. Here the Harper laments that even in solitude he is pursued by anguish: if only I can once be on my own in the grave, he sings, then pain will leave me alone; and the music becomes a noble progression of harped chords in A flat, the home key of the song. Elsewhere, however, the music shows signs of flagging invention caused not so much, it seems, by failing melodic powers as by preconceptions about the harmonic and accompanimental scheme, which prevent the fine opening tune from fulfilling the promise of its first few bars.

The 'Ballade des Harfners' stands apart from the other Harper's songs in being a full-scale ballad along the lines of 'Belsatzar'—one dominated, that is, more than usual with Schumann by musical considerations. It is true that the music itself is not particularly distinguished, for Schumann was understandably less stirred by the purely intellectual idea of art for art's sake ('Ich singe wie der Vogel singt') than by the personal anguish of Mignon and the Harper. Yet once again the wealth of material excites interest to an extent that the illustrative techniques in a ballad such as Schiller's 'Der Handschuh', which Schumann set line by line the following year, never could. In particular the grandeur and pomposity of Goethe's poem is accurately translated into musical terms.

It was perhaps this song in particular, with its suggestion of the harp-player as being in some way connected, through history, with the ideals of heroism and gallantry, that prompted

Schumann to set three more of Byron's *Hebrew Melodies* with harp accompaniment in December of this year. They form in every way a sad appendix to the Goethe songs. At the best of times Schumann was unresponsive to epic verse, and Byron's 'Jephtha's Daughter' ('Die Tochter Jephta's'), 'To the Moon' ('An den Mond') and 'To the Hero' ('Dem Helden') are in any case hardly superior examples of the genre. In the resulting music, the vocal melodies have a certain archaic grandeur. But Schumann's attempts to free himself from Byron's repetitive metric and rhyming schemes have the ring of moral rather than expressive necessity, and although the songs are more coherent than the Goethe settings, it is at terrible cost to their musical interest. Perhaps the saddest aspect of these songs is the indication they give that Schumann was to prove unable to build on the achievement of the Goethe songs. Everything about op. 95 is conventional, from the interminable arpeggiation of its accompaniments to the massive strophic and cryptostrophic forms, and the stolid rhetoric of its word-setting. Schumann must have been dissatisfied with this work, for he never attempted anything of the kind again. In his last years he wrote a number of ballad-cantatas, one of which, *Des Sängers Fluch*, contains two harp songs that are often included in lists of Schumann's lieder, and it was into these works that he channelled his heroic aspirations. In the solo songs of 1850—as if in reaction—the lyrical impulse begins once more to assert itself.

This was to be an unsettled year for Schumann. Even by 1849 it had become apparent that Dresden held out few prospects of the official appointment so desired for him by Clara, and when in November Ferdinand Hiller, the music director at Düsseldorf, suggested that Schumann should succeed to that post the following year, he was bound to give the idea serious consideration whatever his private misgivings. There was also trouble over the Leipzig production of *Genoveva*, which was to have taken place in February 1850 but was finally postponed in favour of Meyerbeer's *Le Prophète*. What with these and other distractions Schumann wrote nothing else until April, when he began going through some of his old compositions, finalizing versions and perhaps also using up sketches in certain new works. More than one of the songs completed during this month has characteristics which link it with the early 1840 songs, though there is little comparison as to stature. Indeed the thirty or so lieder of 1850 are a miscellaneous, even aimless collection, part-lyrical, part-symphonic, part-dramatic—an uneasy compromise between old and new ideals.

The compromise is seen at its worst in the six songs, op. 89, to poems by Wielfried von der Neun.* Neun's verse is fundamentally lyrical in cut, but like so much German lyric poetry of its day it aspires to spiritual significance through the drawing of would-be profound morals, usually in a final portentously explanatory stanza, in which some aspect of nature is compared with a parallel situation in life. Schumann was impressed by what we should now regard as the sententiousness of such writing, and he gave it suitably imposing music. The first song, 'Es stürmet am Abendhimmel', for instance, is a genuine piece of symphonic storm music in the tradition of Beethoven or early Wagner, closely constructed from the chromatic motive heard in the first two bars of the accompaniment, but completely out of scale with the three short quatrains of the poem. Much the same is true of 'Gesungen', which Schumann omitted from op. 89, but published later as op. 96, no. 4. Two other songs, 'Herbstlied' and 'Röselein, Röselein', use motto themes to help unify settings which otherwise follow their poems too closely for absolute musical safety. 'Herbstlied' is in every way a dismal instance of mechanical, line-by-line setting, barely kept moving by piano semiquavers, the drooping motto theme, and a facile enharmonic change from C sharp minor to D flat major for the last line's promise of future happiness in the sunlit treetops. In 'Röselein, Röselein' Schumann's touch is lighter, mainly because he chooses to ignore the touching moral behind Neun's discovery that all roses have thorns. As so often in the 1840 lyrics the music springs directly from a pianistic idea. But now, instead of adapting the voice to the same music, the composer allows the piano to carry the description while the singer merely comments, like the wondering hero of the poem, returning over and over to the falling fifth of his opening

---

* A pseudonym, which modestly includes its owner among the Nine Muses. His real name was Wilhelm Töpff (or, according to Sams, Schöpff).

invocation. The asymmetry which results has a naturalness rare in late Schumann. Thus, when the poet awakes to a C major version of the piano's original A major music, we accept it not just because it aptly describes the idea of waking to the (only slightly altered) scene of one's dream, but also because the singer's invocation in A minor, the relative of C major, has prepared us musically for the change.

If 'Röselein, Röselein' is the only song of genius among the Neun settings, others are not without a certain sugary charm, notably 'Heimliches Verschwinden', a Mendelssohnian song-without-words no more than loosely derived from the poem, and 'Himmel und Erde' (op. 96, no. 5), a true period piece with its rich plush harmonies and absurdly complacent moral. Rather more characteristic than either are 'Abschied vom Walde', which almost reads like a chromatically elaborated version of 'Hör' ich das Liedchen klingen' (even down to the melancholy *appoggiatura* on the phrase 'Herbstes Melodei'n'— autumn's melodies), and 'Ins Freie', the last in a long line of B flat outdoor marching-songs (discounting the slightly later 'Husarenabzug' and the first 'Husarenlied', op. 117, whose heartiness is rather that of the parade-ground than that of the mountain path). 'Ins Freie' is alone among the Neun songs in adopting the old device of repeating and extending the first verse to allow a formal reprise and coda; 'Himmel und Erde' uses a varied reprise to a new verse of the poem, and 'Gesungen' is strophic. But the tendency is to avoid verse divisions in the interests of organic design. It is at once the most up-to-date and the most unsettling feature of op. 89.

In some of the lyrics of this period, however, Schumann was more content to stand by the ideals of 1840, though he seldom managed to recapture the freshness of 'Jasminenstrauch' or 'Der Nussbaum'. Both Goethe's 'Liebeslied' and Platen's 'Ihre Stimme' (sadly* Schumann's only setting of this important poet) emerge as pale shadows of 'Lied der Suleika', for all their rippling semiquaver accompaniments, while anyone listening to 'Aufträge' is likely to recall Schubert's 'Liebesbotschaft' with regret, as no doubt Schumann was doing when he wrote the

---

* If not surprisingly. The cool classicism of most of Platen's verses was hardly calculated to appeal to the sentimental Schumann.

song. But there is also a distinctive 1850 flower-song manner, smoother and less piquant than that of 1840, but no less elegant in its way. Significantly enough, the best (and best-known) example of this style is a Rückert setting, 'Die Blume der Ergebung'. Its most noticeable characteristic is that, as in all the late songs, the chromaticism is functional rather than colouristic, which means that the music tends to modulate more fluently—and therefore less strikingly—than in earlier songs. 'Die Blume der Ergebung', for instance, floats indecisively from tonic to subdominant to subdominant relative minor, for no reason to be found in the poem, and its appeal is more general—that of a shapely vocal melody and an accompaniment which sits well and moves easily. In 'Geisternähe' and 'Frühlingslust', on the other hand, the chromaticism has become superfluous, serving neither a functional purpose nor —except in the sense that it disguises a fundamental dullness in the harmony—a decorative one. 'Frühlingslust' is saved by an attractive tune and a well-ventilated accompaniment, but 'Geisternähe' shows only the dangers of a Mendelssohnian drawing-room style without the benefit of Mendelssohn's supreme craftsmanship.

At its worst Schumann's chromatic late style was capable of extravagances scarcely less than astonishing for the composer of 'Im wunderschönen Monat Mai'. In 'Resignation' the thick, treacly harmonies are unrelieved by any sense of consistent purpose in either melody or accompaniment, so that the song sticks fast—as indeed treacle should. Yet more static is the slightly later 'Stiller Vorwurf', which has all the characteristics of an operatic recitative except the most important one, drama; it is one of the comparatively few Schumann songs which call to mind Wagner. Even in fairy ballads like 'Schneeglöckchen' (op. 96, no. 2) and 'Die Meerfee', the composer seems temporarily to have lost his ability to propel a song without over-elaboration. 'Schneeglöckchen' resembles some of the Neun songs in its line-by-line correspondence with the anonymous text, yet for all its vivid and variegated detail the music never moves freely. Mendelssohnian prettiness without Mendelssohn's expertise is again a culprit in both songs.

A more significant factor, however, is the poverty of the texts set, for Schumann can still be relied on to respond intuitively to the underlying character of a poem, and if—as is the case with 'Schneeglöckchen'—the verse is common-place, the imagery diffuse and the meaning unclear, these qualities will usually be reflected in the music. The point is underlined by other songs of 1850. Ferdinand Braun's 'Frühlingslied', for instance, is a sweet, unpretentious lyric (if we ignore, as Schumann does, the cautionary moral) from which emerges a child's song worthy of the best of its kind in the *Liederalbum für die Jugend*. In Hoffmann von Fallersleben's 'Mein Garten', by contrast, the sententious point of the verse is in the composer's mind from the start, hence the self-conscious solemnity of the music, its surprising failure to paint the scene, and the otherwise inexplicable move to F major (from A minor) at the saddest part of the poem—'only the flower of happiness will you *not* find in my garden'. But the most spectacular example is Goethe's 'Über allen Gipfeln ist Ruh', which Schubert set as 'Wanderers Nachtlied' and Schumann simply as 'Nachtlied'. The poem is surely one of the great lyric epigrams in any language, a distillation in four-and-twenty words of the timeless peace of the universe and the smallness of human anxieties. Schumann's music is immediately alive to its simplicity and nobility without rhetoric. The broad diatonic opening—almost motionless—the sudden change to mysterious chromatics at the word 'Hauch' ('breath') and the contrary-motion triplet chords framing the words 'only wait' (a wonderful moment of expectancy):

all these are sparing gestures calculated to a nicety. Only in the postlude does Schumann perhaps yield momentarily to rhetoric, and if his song is inferior to Schubert's it is at this point alone.

'Nachtlied' is not the only attempt at a mystical utterance through simple diatonic harmony among the 1850 songs. 'Der Einsiedler', a lesser setting of a lesser, but by no means unimpressive, poem by Eichendorff, shares its nature in both subject and musical style. With this substantially longer poem, however, Schumann made the mistake of avoiding chromatics almost entirely, and although there are some unusual, even memorable, progressions within the limits of plain D minor they cannot sustain interest for three unaltered verses. A rather different case is that of Strachwitz's 'Mein altes Ross', Schumann's setting of which starts in the vein of 'Der Einsiedler' but broadens out into an elaborate straight-through setting whose piano figuration owes something to the much-admired Schubert of the piano sonatas. The song ends better than it begins. The march rhythm of the opening is puzzling if we are to assume that the heartbroken poet is on horseback, and the word-setting is square—unusually so for late Schumann. But both features evaporate in the more intricate rhythms and harmonies of the development, and when the march returns over a throbbing, dominant pedal, it has the force of a threnody, a comment rather than a description.

Schumann's last songs composed in Dresden were the Lenau cycle, op. 90; six settings of poems by Lenau, and the 'Requiem' added in memory of the poet, who died in August. Lenau was a peculiarly sympathetic figure to Schumann. By 1850 he had spent five years in an asylum, but even before that his mental instability had found outlet in a number of profoundly depressive lyrics whose mood echoes the melancholia Schumann himself experienced from time to time, and with increasing frequency after his marriage. However, not all the Lenau poems he set are from this category. Op. 90 is in fact a miscellany of four love-songs (three of them depressive), a rather autumnal cow-girl's song, and a thoroughly cheerful blacksmith's song, plus the consolatory 'Requiem'. True, the seven songs are arranged in key sequence, but this was by now more or less a habit with Schumann. Where three of the songs —'Kommen und Scheiden', 'Die Sennin', and 'Einsamkeit'— follow a more involved tonal pattern we can look for some connection between them and discover that they are indeed all about loneliness. But it is not to be considered that the composer regarded the whole cycle as being linked in any such way.

Individually the songs are less ambitious than the earlier Neun songs, and also more varied. There is nothing in op. 89 so simply effective as 'Lied eines Schmiedes', so narrowly chromatic as 'Kommen und Scheiden', or so naive as 'Die Sennin', with its persistent *ranz des vaches*. But Lenau's greater economy and sharper perceptions also raised problems which the Schumann of 1850 was no longer well equipped to solve. An obvious instance is 'Meine Rose', where, instead of trying to match the neat, if rather insipid, metaphor which the poem's two verses draw between the wilting rose and the wilting love, the composer allows himself to be hypnotized by the scene, repeats the first verse at the end, and so destroys the whole point of the poem. 'Die Sennin' is another poem whose symmetry—this time expressed as a contrast between the joy of the cow-girl's presence and the sorrow of her absence— deserves more pointed musical realization than a rather mechanical change from B major to D sharp major, which is in any case a comparatively bright modulation. However, both these songs have a creative freshness which is wholly lacking in the depressive love-songs, 'Kommen und Scheiden', 'Einsamkeit', and 'Der schwere Abend'. The poems are distinguished by their unrelieved gloom and pessimism. 'Der schwere Abend' is set as a virtual rerun of 'Ich hab' im Traum geweinet', in the same louring E flat minor and with the same accompaniment figure. But the heavy, nerveless textures, the very image of death, are in marked contrast with the jabbing monosyllables of the earlier song, where grief was essentially the pain of waking and living. The most remarkable of these songs is 'Einsamkeit', also in E flat minor but with warmer passages in B minor and E flat major as the poet gropes unconvincingly for comfort in his loneliness. As in 'O Freund, mein Schirm, mein Schutz', the almost reckless use of passing-note dissonance seems to spring from Bach, though the figuration is characteristic of Schumann and recalls 'Zwielicht' and 'Muttertraum'. One can well understand that in 1850 a song of this kind might be thought excessively modern, and its composer well on the way to insanity.

But Schumann was not yet ready for certification, and in

'Requiem' he clearly and deliberately drew back from the abyss, renouncing the despair of 'Der schwere Abend'. The music, like the gesture, is synthetic, full of the counterfeit serenity of angels' harps and church organs, and lacking the conviction of its exorcistic predecessors, 'Frühlingsnacht' and 'Die alten, bösen Lieder'. But if the failure seems significant, the irony is greater, for Lenau was not yet dead when his obituary was composed. It was, the superstitious Schumann wrote later, 'as though I were unwittingly tolling a passing bell'. No doubt the more frightening personal significance of the error was also not entirely lost on him.

6 *Winter*

Early in September 1850, Schumann's fears about the Düsseldorf appointment having been sufficiently allayed, the couple left Dresden for the Rhine. Robert's health was already giving cause for concern, but seems to have improved after their arrival in Düsseldorf. The Rhenish Symphony, composed in November, certainly gives no indication of having been written under handicap, and there were other compositions in the autumn and early winter, notably the Cello Concerto. By the time he returned to song-writing in January 1851, however, his style had undergone a distinct, even radical, change. In the final songs, composed over a period of almost two years, barely a trace remains of the maudlin, overripe chromaticism of the weaker 1850 lyrics, nor is there much sign of the visionary calm of 'Nachtlied' or the more pretentious grandeur of the Neun songs. Indeed pretence of all kinds is banished from these songs. In its place is a simple expression of emotion—no longer the emotion of a young and excitable lover, as in *Dichterliebe*, but the quieter, more introspective feelings of a prematurely ailing man of forty.

Many interpretations have been put on this very real change of emphasis in Schumann's writing. It is common to see in the songs a symptom of the mental decline already apparent in his day-to-day behaviour, and no doubt this is right—insofar as it implies no blanket judgement of the music's artistic value or interest. Wolf's songs are the work of a madman, but this only helps define the word 'madman', not to evaluate Wolf's songs. In 1851 Schumann was very far from insane in the popular sense of the term. But he was certainly getting vaguer and more detached, a process which had indeed been going on since his marriage; the composer of the 1851–2 songs was a shier, more self-communing, more outwardly placid individual than the composer of the *Wilhelm Meister* or even the Lenau songs of the previous two years.

This lack of excitability or 'temperament' is a major

difficulty of Schumann's late music. It hangs like a deadweight around his last choral works and the few orchestral works (mostly overtures) of the period, and it can mislead the casual listener into dismissing the songs *en bloc* as dull or uneventful. Certainly many of them lack the expressive range of their predecessors, and technically they are often diffuse and muddled. But Schumann spent the greater part of his creative life struggling with a limited compositional technique. The effects of his symphonic and operatic work on the songs of 1849–50 were often little short of disastrous, and it is hardly surprising that a year or so later he had still not solved the problem of working with differentiated material in a confined musical space. Much of the rhythmic obtuseness of the late songs arises from his inability to revert to that economical use of material which typifies the best songs of 1840. Where he succeeds in doing so, as in 'Herzeleid', the result can be almost painfully moving, not less because the language in which it is couched is essentially depressive and repetitive. It can also, it must be admitted, be pale and lifeless; the seven Elisabeth Kulmann songs, op. 104, are a terrible warning of the level to which music can sink when its composer allows sincerity of feeling to stand in place of musical invention.

Throughout this final period Schumann's songs are content with a plainer idiom than he had used (other than in op. 79) since 1840, but one quite unlike the stripped style of the early Heine settings. Even in the Kulmann songs, where he deliberately recreates the chaperoned simplicity of the poetry, the tunes have the simpering childishness of a young girl who has been taught that simpleness is next to saintliness. They altogether lack the straightforwardness of 'Morgens steh' ich auf' or, on a lower plane, the better children's songs in op. 79. In the other late songs, tunes in this sense hardly occur at all. Rather are the words set as a kind of free *arioso*, or even as plain recitative, the vocal phrases being placed irregularly over—or occasionally in dialogue with—the accompaniment. This technique is obviously a legacy of Schumann's dramatic works, and it occurs in many songs of 1849, most notably the Goethe settings. But in the Düsseldorf songs there is no longer any hint of declamation or music theatre. Instead the music, like the man, has become reflective and introverted, the expression cramped almost to the point of ellipsis. In 1852 Schumann began, for the first time in his life, to take an interest in religion and religious music. But except in the Mary Stuart settings, op. 135, composed in December 1852, there is no sign of this in the songs, where self-pity is the predominant emotion.

Harmonically the Düsseldorf songs have an astringency only occasionally to be found in those written in Dresden. Schumann seems to have tired of the cloying effect of songs like 'Ihre Stimme' or 'Himmel und Erde', with their rich, fulsome chromaticism. The last songs are chromatic enough, in their way; but the dissonance is normally arrived at by counterpoint —that is, by the movement of individual lines in the texture in relation to one another—rather than by the piling-up of chords or the sliding of one harmony into the next. 'Herzeleid' is a good example of a linear technique which clearly owes something to Bach. The whole character of this mournful song is conditioned by the right-hand piano melody, which gropes its way from semitone to semitone oblivious of the accented discords (minor seconds and ninths and major sevenths) generated against the more picturesque left-hand semiquavers:

Apart from a few isolated chords, the spare texture of these two conflicting strands dominates the song, while the singer enters listlessly from time to time in an irregular pattern of phrases, a demented witness of his own (rather than Ophelia's) suicide. The whole effect is almost unbearably poignant, not least because the actual harmonies move only from E minor to C major (the subdominant relative major, a bitter-sweet progression) and back again.

In fact no less than sixteen of the twenty-seven songs composed from January 1851 are in minor keys, an astonishing proportion when one remembers that even in *Dichterliebe* only half the songs are in the minor, while in *Myrten* the figure is seven out of twenty-six. Of course the minor mode is not in itself necessarily the bearer of bad tidings. Two of Schumann's earliest minor-key songs, 'Schlusslied des Narren' and 'Setze mir nicht', are both comic pieces. But in the later songs the use of minor keys is definitely depressive, if not always as morbidly so as in 'Herzeleid'. The other Titus Ulrich setting, 'Die Fensterscheibe', for example, retains at least a memory of the coquettish quality of Schumann's earlier soubrette songs, 'Die Kartenlegerin' and 'Singet nicht in Trauertönen', in the gentle lilt of its vocal melody. But there is certainly no suggestion that this window-cleaner is anything but a figure of sadness. Her fate is clear from the very first bar of the piano introduction, where Schumann leans hard on the minor sixth, seventh and ninth:

and from later piano interludes, where flattened supertonic harmony (chords of C major still in B minor), and again the minor sixth, lend the music a specially piquant air of melancholy. Curiously enough the more conventionally chromatic passages in this song, as for instance at 'da geht er stolz vorbei', are much less painful in effect.

This predominance of certain intervals and chords in relation to the keynote is a feature of Schumann's handling of minor keys in his late songs. The minor second and sixth are invariably instruments of torture in this, as in much other romantic music, and when they occur in isolation, without fulfilling their proper chromatic function of helping the music into a new key, the effect can be peculiarly desolate and despairing. For instance, in 'Im Wald', a generally unremarkable setting of a poem about loneliness by Wolfgang Müller, even the most casual listener is likely to be made aware that at the recurrent words 'ich bin so allein voll Pein', with its drooping F naturals against the keynote A and dominant E, Schumann is speaking—not without bitterness—about himself. The even more comfortless 'Die Spinnerin' transmutes this same relationship into an appropriate spinning-wheel figure which, like the right-hand melody in 'Herzeleid', goes right through the song oblivious of the rending discords it sets up with the voice part (see especially the clashes on 'Rädchen' and, at the end, 'ich weiss es ja nicht'). Here too there is a hint of bitterness, in for instance the setting of the word 'lustig' ('merry'—the other girls, that is) for which Schumann finds an ironic minor sixth and a sudden *forte-piano* in the accompaniment.

The best-known songs of loneliness from this period are the five Mary Stuart settings, op. 135, with which Schumann closed his song-writing career in December 1852.* By this stage he was clearly choosing poetry purely for its relevance to his own inner fears, the fear of death and the living oblivion of incarceration, and perhaps not least the terrible suspicion, barely overlaid by the religious leanings of his music at this time, that trust in the next world was nothing more than the last resort of those who had lost all hope in this. Some such feeling, at least, is present in the two overtly religious songs of op. 135, 'Nach der Geburt ihres Sohnes' and 'Gebet', which for all the devoutness of their texts speak in musical terms only of the profoundest unyielding despair. Significantly four of the five songs, including these two, are in E minor, the key of 'Herzeleid'—a remarkable confession, by a composer so sensitive to key contrasts, that his mind has come to be dominated by a single mood.

The exception is 'An die Königin Elisabeth', which is in A minor, a concession perhaps to the 'Hoffnung' in the poem's third line. This is also musically the most interesting of the five. Like many of Schumann's late songs it has a hybrid form, starting with two verses composed strophically but then continuing in free form to the end. In performance, however, the music tends to sound entirely fluid, because the vocal line is composed

---

* The poems, originally in Latin, are only putatively by Mary Stuart, Queen of Scots, who was executed by order of Queen Elizabeth I in 1587. The German translations are by Gisbert Freiherr von Vincke.

as in tempo recitative, while the accompaniment has a distinctly symphonic freedom of movement (some of its material in fact strongly resembles the main first movement subject of the Second Symphony). The result, if not inspired, is highly accomplished, perhaps the nearest Schumann came—albeit on a miniature scale—to an integrated symphonic style of writing.

Of the other two songs, 'Abschied von der Welt' falls somewhere between the pure chordal-recitative style of 'Gebet' and the more enterprising 'symphonic' manner of 'An die Königin Elisabeth'. 'Abschied von Frankreich', on the other hand, is a straightforward art-song after 'Herzeleid', though its ascending semiquaver arpeggios are more conventional than the descending ones of the earlier song. Once again the music's appeal lies in its undemonstrative insistence on a mood of utter misery broken only by nostalgic backward glances to a past that was at least slightly less unhappy. In 'Abschied von Frankreich' such moments are both more frequent and more varied than in 'Herzeleid', but it is noticeable that when writing in major keys Schumann now lapses more readily into triviality and cliché. No doubt this also partly explains the growing incidence of minor keys in his Düsseldorf songs.

This is not to say, however, that the major-key songs of 1851 are without musical value. On the contrary, as regards invention they contain some of the best of late Schumann, though inevitably their quality is somewhat unequal. Even the Schumann of 1840 would have been hard pressed to make anything more arresting of Pfarrius's 'Die Hütte' than the overelaborate recomposition of 'Freisinn' which begins op. 119. On the other hand the failure of 'Der Bräutigam und die Birke' is disappointing, for the poem suggests obvious possibilities for a lively musical game. The composer of 'Die Kartenlegerin' ought, one feels, to have achieved something less laboured here. Some idea of the difficulties Schumann now seems to have faced in marshalling his creative ideas can however be gauged by an examination of the two Mörike settings of this period, 'Jung Volkers Lied' and 'Der Gärtner', both composed in January 1851.

The song of the robber Jung Volker is part folk-pastiche, part character-sketch, but Schumann concentrates mainly on the latter aspect and attempts a swift line-drawing in the manner of 'Der Hidalgo'. But his muscles have lost their co-ordination and the lines never meet. Thus no musical connection is ever established between the rushing semiquaver figures in the accompaniment (representing Volker's supposed father, the wind) and the disjointed fragments of tune sung, often unaccompanied, by the voice, while the galloping piano figure which intervenes between them is notable mainly for its complete irrelevance to either. Not surprisingly, with such an array of conflicting ideas, no amount of breeze or bluster can hide the underlying confusion of the thought. A similar confusion exists in 'Der Gärtner' but it is less damaging. Here Schumann is able to confine himself to a single musical image, the idea of the princess's horse prancing along the avenue; and the piano figure with which he represents this:

is so perfect that we see the whole scene at once: the shimmering dream-beauty of the girl, the snow-white horse leaping forward or holding back, even the glittering sand which the gardener strews across the path like gold-dust. Unfortunately the figure has such rhythmic subtlety that the composer finds it hard to work the voice part tidily against it. In any but the most accomplished performance the music can seem fussy and over-composed. But in an accomplished—which is to say delicately understated—performance, it is one of Schumann's gems.

'Der Gärtner' is one of the most diatonic of the late songs. Though it uses chromaticism, and changes key freely, its essence lies in the bell-like resonance of primary triads in root position. In this it resembles 'Abendlied'—and not in this only, for the setting of Gottfried Kinkel's poem suffers from the same rhythmic imbalance as the Mörike song. Once again Schumann discovers a perfect musical image for the poem's central idea, the stillness of night acting as balm for human anxieties, and the swaying piano triplets hold the imagination only to have the spell broken when the voice enters with a cross-rhythm which persists for most of the song. In spite of the maddening over-complexity which results, 'Abendlied' is nevertheless a beautiful song. As he had done in his setting of Goethe's 'Nachtlied', Schumann glimpsed the mystery, as well as the silence, of deep night, and captured both in his music, failing only in the attempt to fuse the two. Incidentally, Mahler seems to have known and admired 'Abendlied': a passage from it (at the words 'wirf ab, Herz, was dich kränket') is quoted almost note-for-note in the soprano's 'O glaube; du wardst nicht umsonst geboren!' in the finale of his Second Symphony, with the same idea of redemption from worldly cares.

The Lenau songs of 1851 stand somewhat apart from the others of that year on account of their curiously incongruous subject-matter. Altogether five Lenau settings date from the last period, but of these 'Frühlingsgrüsse' (another song characterized by cross-rhythms) was not published by Schumann.* The other four are the *Husarenlieder*, op. 117. It is not clear why the sensitive and retiring Schumann should suddenly have turned to this bloodthirsty poetry for musical setting. Admittedly he had shown a fondness in the past for musical militaristics, but always there had been an element either of toy soldiery ('Soldatenlied') or of pathos ('Der Soldat'). Even in 'Husarenabzug', a song full of praise for the 'merry lads' of the cavalry, music is little more than a parade-ground display of brightly polished bugles and guns cleaned but not loaded. But in the *Husarenlieder* it is the real thing. The soldiers in these poems chafe at peace, rejoice at war, and relish all things bloody or blood-red; and if there is protest in Lenau's verses it is not apparent to the English reader, and was not apparent to Schumann.

The settings (for bass voice) are direct, like the poems, and although they display some of the faults of overelaboration found in other songs of this period, they contain much that is fine. The best song is the second, 'Der leidige Frieden', which uses an *ostinato* rhythm with powerful effect to convey a sense

---

* Like 'Ein Gedanke' (see footnote p. 30) it was published in the *Musical Quarterly* of January 1942.

of repressed energy, bursting out suddenly in the furious blood-letting of the final verse. 'Der Husar, trara!' is really nothing more than a vigorous and compact version of 'Husarenabzug', with which it shares its strophic form. The other two songs are of interest rather for technical details than for their general effect. 'Den grünen Zeigern' suffers, like an earlier Lenau setting, 'Meine Rose', from one of Schumann's gratuitous first-verse repeats, which spoils the poet's antithesis between the athletics of peace and war. In *Da liegt der Feinde* the spectre of cross-rhythm once again looms to threaten a song which depends largely on the impetus generated by the (rather Schubertian) unison triplet figure of its opening bars.

With these twenty-six songs Schumann's career as a songwriter comes to an end. As with most categories of his music, it is essentially a sad end—sad both in the character of the music itself, and because its quality, though sometimes good, cannot equal that of earlier work. But those who believe that Schumann's late songs are of greater pathological than musical interest should think again, for at the age of forty-one, and entering a mental decline, he was still turning out original, thoughtful and occasionally inspired work. What his late music lacks is that element of concentration which makes *Dichterliebe* one of the great works of romantic art. In the inspired songs of 1849–52 his genius leaps from idea to idea so rapidly that the organizing parts of his mind cannot always keep up. But the genius is there still. Only those who hold that life is too short for the enjoyment of anything but flawless masterpieces will find nothing in these songs to stimulate their imagination.

7   The Song-writer

Any attempt to assess Schumann's total achievement as a song-writer should begin at source, with the poets whose work he set to music. It has often been said that, with the exception of Wolf, Schumann was the most discriminating of the great lieder composers in his choice of texts. It would perhaps be truer to say that he was the most orthodox. Brought up in a literary atmosphere, he automatically chose Shakespeare, Goethe, Heine, Burns and Byron for his earliest songs in 1840; later Eichendorff, Rückert, Lenau, Kerner and Chamisso—all poets of repute at the time he set them—are the most regular additions to that list. But to judge a poem by its poet is a dangerous activity, and the truth is that Schumann's choice of texts by these authors will not always bear close examination. Leaving aside the one insignificant Shakespeare setting, only Heine, Eichendorff and (with allowance for the translations) Burns could afford to stake much of their reputations on the verse selected by Schumann. The Goethe poems set in 1840 are of little account, and the composer can hardly be applauded for his personal good taste in later setting the *Wilhelm Meister* songs, which were on every nineteenth-century song-writer's lips. Rückert, Lenau and Chamisso are barely more than nonentities judged by Schumann's selection. Admittedly modern taste is not sympathetic to a facile lyricist of Rückert's type; but there are many stronger things in Rückert than Schumann's choice from the *Liebesfrühling*, as both Schubert and Mahler knew. On the other hand, Schumann had a disconcerting fondness for the worst kind of sentimental or pretentious romantic lyric, and even if we discount his settings of Neun or the child poet Elisabeth Kulmann as the aberrations of a failing mind, it is hard to explain away the Reinick songs or such pieces as 'Der Himmel hat eine Träne geweint' or 'Nur ein lächelnder Blick', all composed in 1840–1.

Not literary taste but literary instinct was Schumann's

special quality as a song-writer. Perhaps no composer has had such an ability to sense the underlying qualities of a poem and reproduce them in music. This was not a conscious gift; had it been so, then it might have influenced his taste. Instead, as we have seen, it worked impartially on the worst poetry and the best. The Kulmann songs are too extreme an example to be typical, but the Neun songs reflect much of the confusion between lyric expression and portentous moralizing which characterizes the verse—even while Schumann, in his conscious mind, was clearly impressed by the poet's blending of these qualities. At the other end of the scale, the settings of Heine, Burns, Eichendorff and Chamisso all show the power words had to influence the sort of music Schumann composed. Goethe too drew heavily on this faculty. Schumann was not really a big enough thinker to control the music the *Wilhelm Meister* poems inspired him to write, but the earlier Goethe songs unfailingly catch the essence of the poems, if not of the poet. Of course, there are exceptions. 'Der Nussbaum' is a sickly poem but a delicately elusive song, while on the other hand 'Das verlassene Mägdelein' and 'Er ist's' both fall short of the perfection of Mörike's verse. Schumann occasionally also missed specific points that fell outside his psychological compass; his settings of Heine often, as in 'Berg und Burgen' and 'Die Lotosblume', miss the sharp sting of the closing line or stanza, though the quality of irony is well caught in 'Wenn ich in deine Augen seh'', and even created where it barely existed in such a poem as 'Die Grenadiere'. Any kind of wit or comedy was likely to leave Schumann well in the rear. 'Setze mir nicht' and 'Die Kartenlegerin' are rare instances of genuine humour in his songs, while 'Schlusslied des Narren', 'Rätsel', and worst of all 'Der Contrabandiste' are all notable failures in this department. His frequent failure to recreate drama in song was perhaps technical as much as psychological. In 'Belsatzar' one feels that the drama is perceived but not realized, and later 'Der Handschuh' is a remarkable instance of a dramatic text converted into music with all its theatrical detail intact but its drama lost. Yet even here distinguished exceptions give us pause: 'Der Schatzgräber' and 'Muttertraum' are genuine, if small-scale, music dramas, and *Dichterliebe* itself is a perfect lyric drama which succeeds because the 'plot' consists not of action but of psychological reaction. In this field, Schumann was in a class of his own.

But for all his skill at recreating the atmosphere or hidden spirit of a poem, Schumann was often an unscrupulous word-setter. In song after song he quite simply misquotes his source, sometimes inexplicably, as when he substitutes 'Kerker' ('prison') for Eichendorff's 'Käfig' ('cage') in 'Wehmut'. Almost a whole line is left out of the middle of 'Er ist's', and in another Mörike song, 'Jung Volkers Lied', a flurry of misquotes includes the amusing 'Mutterarm' for 'Mutterleib . Other errors, such as the repetition of 'Pein instead of 'Qual' in 'Wer sich der Einsamkeit ergibt', are clearly slips of the pen. More serious, because involving the substance of the music, is Schumann's fondness for repetition of lines or verses. In this he had a distinguished exemplar in Schubert. But there are few repetitions in Schubert so disastrous as Schumann's verse repeats in 'Meine Rose' or 'Schöne Wiege meiner Leiden', which destroy antitheses in the poems, or the astonishingly insensitive stretching-out of 'Er ist's', or the grand declamatory reprise in 'Stille Tränen', a virtual admission of the disparities between the verse and its music. On such occasions Schumann's instincts seem to have completely deserted him. But not all such repeats are damaging. 'Widmung' and 'Lied der Suleika' are good examples of essentially static or reflective poems where no harm results from the procedure, and in 'Intermezzo', as we have seen, the repeat is justified by the sense of homecoming in the music. Perhaps the best example of all is 'Ich grolle nicht', where a deliberate change in the sense of the poem requires repeats of the title words for emphasis. The result may not be what Heine meant, but it makes a fine and psychologically right effort.

Schumann has sometimes been criticized for faulty or inaccurate scansion, but this seems a less valid point. Music creates its own rhythms, and it can be a far worse fault for a composer to follow those of his source poem slavishly, as Schumann does in many of his weakest songs ('Sonntags am Rhein', 'Die Nonne', and the majority of his ballads), though also in some of his greatest ('Hör' ich das Liedchen klingen', 'Und wüssten's die Blumen', 'Jasminenstrauch'), where a surface simplicity is particularly sought. Occasionally the scansion is changed for the simple reason that the verse has to be fitted into preconceived piano music, as seems to be happening in 'Leis' rudern hier'. But in later life Schumann became more conscious of the positive advantages of free, unscanned word-setting, and this is a feature of the late Goethe and Byron songs and almost all the Düsseldorf songs. Even in a superficially plain setting such as 'Lied eines Schmiedes' the poet's scansion is completely altered with no loss of rhythmic character or strength.

Declamation is on the whole good in Schumann's early songs, though here too his tendency to conceive his music in terms of the piano sometimes ran him into difficulties when it came to fitting the text to the tune. 'Mit Myrten und Rosen' is a weak, rather than positively bad, example of words and music indifferently matched. Another is 'Waldesgespräch', with its awkward snatch on 'Es ist schon spät'. But actual wrong stress is uncommon among the 1840 songs. There is a glaring example in 'Was soll ich sagen!', where the contrast between 'mein' and 'dein' is missed. But the Chamisso songs as a whole are a model of just accentuation. One of the reasons for the popularity of *Frauenliebe und -leben* is its fine, even word-setting, which singers appreciate, and the same is true (though its popularity hardly depends on this) of *Dichterliebe*. In later life Schumann was often less considerate, and at its worst his forgetfulness could produce absurd anomalies, as in 'So lasst mich scheinen', where the most prominent stresses are on insignificant words like 'dann', 'doch' and 'auf'. But more often there is merely a general air of laxity, parallel to the much freer, less purposeful, use of chromatics and dissonance in the later songs.

With few exceptions, Schumann's best songs show that his main interest in setting a poem was to recreate its general psychological atmosphere, rather than necessarily to translate the words into exact musical equivalents. His attitude to word-painting or *Tonmalerei* was thus equivocal. At his best he was always alive to the special significance of key words, as in 'Wenn ich in deine Augen seh' ', or at the words 'trauriger, blasser Mann' in 'Am leuchtenden Sommermorgen'. But such things, he was well aware, are commonplaces of word-setting, as easy to compose as they are to analyse. Of much greater importance is general figuration, for it is this which sets the harmonic and textural character of the song and thus determines its truth or otherwise to the poem as a whole. Coming to song as a habitual piano composer, Schumann found it difficult to break away from the idea of a piano piece with added voice. The whole of op. 24 is basically piano music, and so is at least half of *Myrten*, though admittedly songs where the music is absolutely complete in the piano part—as in 'Hochländisches Wiegenlied' and 'Niemand'—are rather less common. To find this fault at all in Schumann is intriguing, for he was critical of it in other composers. 'It is,' he wrote in a review of some songs by Kufferath, 'certainly no merit in lieder composition, and particularly restricting for the singer.' In time he to some extent eradicated it from his own songs, but it persistently crept back, and there are examples from every period: 'Wehmut', 'Es leuchtet meine Liebe', 'Seit ich ihn gesehen', 'Die Nonne', 'Das verlassene Mägdelein', 'Die wandelnde Glocke', 'Hoch, hoch sind die Berge', 'Im Wald'. The trouble with most of these songs is that their relevance to the words is vague, even where they catch the general atmosphere. Even 'Ich wandelte unter den Bäumen' loses something by its failure to differentiate between piano and vocal material.

In the Eichendorff songs, Schumann at last found his way out of the impasse through the use of characteristic or *ostinato* figuration. He was helped by the underlying sense of allegory in the poems, which allowed a simple recurring figure to be used for both descriptive and psychological ends, as in 'Schöne Fremde' and 'Frühlingsnacht'. Such descriptive figuration is rare in the earlier songs and Schumann theorized about this too, feeling that Schubert had overused the technique, with his archetypal water and spinning-wheel figures. But Schumann himself soon learnt to use figuration as a unifying device in piano parts that were genuinely accompanimental. At least ten of the *Dichterliebe* songs are of this type, though the piano-writing here is generally more economical and always more telling than in any other songs by Schumann. A good instance is 'Ich will meine Seele tauchen', whose rippling demisemiquavers seem to express the idea of the lily's tremulous chalice while also lending a more general sense of tearful sadness. Like most of the Heine and Eichendorff settings, the song is too short for the figure to become monotonous. But Schumann was not always so lucky. For every song in his late period where figurative writing is aptly and sparingly used, as in 'Der Sandmann', 'Röselein, Röselein', or 'Frühlingslust', there is one where it goes on for too long, or is merely a general device with no special relevance to the poem. 'Aufträge', 'Requiem', and most of the other harp songs are of the first type; 'Die Blume der Ergebung' and 'Abschied von Frankreich' of the second. The alternative was often plain chordal accompaniments, and here too Schumann was not always discriminating. If the chords in 'Nachtlied', 'Auf das Trinkglas eines verstorbenen Freundes' or 'Der Einsiedler' are on the whole the chords of a genius, those in 'Blondels Lied', 'Auf dem Rhein' and 'Ins Freie' are merely drab. And repeated chords, so finely effective in 'Ich grolle nicht' and 'Du bist wie eine Blume', soon become a mannerism. *Frauenliebe und -leben* is, as we have seen, beset with them, and there are later examples in 'Sehnsucht' and 'Himmel und Erde', as well as 'Kennst du das Land?', where they are partly saved, however, by their harmonic richness.

Taken as a whole, the *Wilhelm Meister* songs differ from most of Schumann's lieder in the strongly orchestral character of their piano parts. 'Heiss' mich nicht reden' is a good example of a song obviously conceived as a dramatic scena with orchestral accompaniment and a symphonic texture. But even in the Harper's songs, the harp itself is only one component of a rich fabric of sound, while Philine's 'Singet nicht in Trauertönen' cries out for the deftness of strings and woodwind. Schumann did not persevere with this type of accompaniment, though traces of it remain in some of the Neun songs 'Es stürmet am Abendhimmel', 'Herbstlied', 'Gesungen'. A more consistent feature of his piano-writing is the single or double melodic strand which weaves through the texture like a baroque counterpoint. In the 1840 songs this device is used sparingly, and always to create an atmosphere of doubt or fear, as in 'Aus den *Hebräischen Gesängen*', 'Zwielicht', and 'Muttertraum'. But after his Bach studies of 1845, Schumann made much freer use of such writing and its associated dissonance techniques. 'Das verlassene Mägdelein' is an almost pure piece of three-part instrumental counterpoint, while later songs ('O Freund, mein Schirm, mein Schutz', 'Einsamkeit') go to extravagant lengths to create a tortured atmosphere by contrapuntal means. As late as 1851, Schumann still had this image of fear in his system. The Pfarrius song, 'Warnung', deploys, like 'Einsamkeit', a single descending quaver figure (now syncopated) to suggest the onset of night in both the real and figurative senses; so persistent is the metaphor that in a song of only twenty-nine bars night falls no less than eighteen times.

Schumann's greatest contribution to the art of lieder accompaniment lay in his use of the piano postlude. He did not, of course, invent this device. Schubert alone had used it extensively. But in Schubert the postlude is merely a way of finishing the song tidily and effectively, and more often than not it consists of a repeat (modified or otherwise) of the prelude. One would not expect to find in Schubert, as one does in Schumann's 'Und wüssten's die Blumen', an important postlude based on entirely new material. Schumann's postludes, like the rest of his accompanimental technique, are the natural offshoot of his early experience as a composer and improviser at the piano, and in early songs like 'Es treibt mich hin' or 'Schöne Wiege meiner Leiden' we hear this in the way the piano suddenly takes wing in the closing bars, almost as if the composer has been waiting for this moment to get properly to grips with the point of the song. In more than half the songs of this first period the piano has some significant comment to make after the voice has finished, though there are also interesting examples of the opposite device in 'Lieb' Liebchen' and 'Lied der Braut' (II) where a vocal phrase overhangs the final piano chord, as a kind of afterthought. Schumann's greatest postludes are in *Dichterliebe*, and it is here, in song after song, that we hear piano and voice in that true synthesis which Schumann himself believed to be the ideal in song-writing. One of the clearest examples is 'Im wunderschönen Monat Mai', where the groping, ambiguous piano harmonies—unresolved even in the postlude—show the underlying insecurity of the voice's superficially innocent tune. But one might quote several other examples: 'Wenn ich in deine Augen seh' ', with its drooping subdominant close; 'Ich grolle nicht', where the apparently conventional quaver chords well up in an outburst of dismissive anger; 'Das ist ein Flöten und Geigen', with its winding, sardonic 'flute and violin' tune; and 'Die alten, bösen Lieder', where the postlude of 'Am leuchtenden Sommermorgen' returns to confirm the beauty of what is past and the numbed tranquillity of the present. This perfect balancing of expressive functions is achieved with increasing rarity after *Dichterliebe*, though often attempted. In *Frauenliebe und -leben* the postludes are more beautiful than penetrating, and the final return to the music of the opening song has a definite air of contrivance. A more subtle postlude is that of 'Märzveilchen':

which delicately underlines the sad elusiveness of springtime love; and there is another instance, perhaps even more touching, in the wistful music which follows each verse of 'Erstes Grün'. But just as *Dichterliebe* had (or almost had) its 'Mein Wagen rollet langsam', where the piano meanders on aimlessly for many bars after the voice has ended, so the Kerner set has its 'Stille Tränen,' with a huge peroration (partly vocal) which merely points up the inflated character of the setting as a whole. In the later songs, postludes occur rather on the Schubertian pattern, without deep psychological undertones. Sometimes, as in 'Nachtlied', they seem to have outlived their usefulness altogether, and even the attractive postlude to 'Der Gärtner' is little more than a relishing of the delightful prancing motive on which the song is based. Possibly the most effective ending in any late Schumann song is that of 'Heiss' mich nicht reden', where the voice has the last word in an accompanied recitative to a repeat of earlier lines of the poem.

Since the piano was clearly seminal in the early 1840 songs, we should expect to find the vocal style of these works growing out of the piano-writing. And so at first it does. Even in those op. 24 songs where the accompaniment reflects but does not exactly duplicate the vocal line ('Morgens steh' ich auf', 'Lieb' Liebchen', 'Berg und Burgen') one cannot be sure whether the tune is really in origin a vocal one. In 'Berg und Burgen, the voice rides the piano texture like a boat rocking on the surface of a river, but the tune is all there, hidden, in the piano part, just as a strong but elusive thread of melody runs through the elaborate textures of the first movement of *Kreisleriana*. However, a new feature of these melodies is their extreme simplicity, amounting at times (as we saw in 'Morgens steh' ich auf') to plainness, yet not merely the plainness of folksong: rather a kind of deliberate vacuity, like the inscrutable expression of a man unwilling to expose himself to further suffering by showing his true emotions. Even in a great song like 'Ich wandelte unter den Bäumen', the melody taken out of context is quite ordinary, and this remains true of many of the *Dichterliebe* songs, where the tunes often express little or nothing without their accompaniments. In *Dichterliebe*, however, there is no question but that the melodies are vocally conceived, as any singer will confirm. The clear explanation is that Schumann deliberately avoided melodic suggestiveness in songs where some deep psychological insight was required; the simpler the tune, the more scope it gave for those barely perceptible moments of pain and illumination through harmony or texture which are a feature of songs like 'Im wunderschönen Monat Mai' and 'Am leuchtenden Sommermorgen'.

This is apparently borne out by those songs of 1840 where melody is all-important: 'Widmung', 'Lied der Suleika', 'Du bist wie eine Blume', 'Dem roten Röslein', 'Er, der Herrlichste von allen', 'Du Ring an meinem Finger', 'Intermezzo', to name only the best examples of good tunes in the traditional sense. In none of these songs is psychological subtlety so important as the creation of a warmly emotional, or in some cases sensual, atmosphere; and all are, significantly, happy songs. In this view, Schumann is not immune to the charge of oversweetness or unctuousness, precisely because of the heart-on-sleeve feeling of the music. 'Lied der Suleika' is certainly one example. But the fault is more common in the later lyrical phase, where sentiment is all too often replaced by sentimentality. 'Ihre Stimme', 'Liebeslied', even the sincerely charming 'Die Blume der Ergebung', all suffer in some measure from the complacency of a too facile lyricism. At its worst this style could dissolve into a glutinous chromaticism, as it does in 'Resignation'. But at this point autonomous melody has virtually ceased to exist, and instead the vocal line is once again simply a projection of the harmony.

The typical melodic style of Schumann's later songs is really a kind of recitative, at its best in the *Wilhelm Meister* songs, where it retains a vestigial connection with the operatic style of *Genoveva*. Some of the free melodic passages in these songs are magnificent: the opening phrase, for instance, of 'Wer sich der Einsamkeit ergibt', or the broad A flat melody at the words 'ach! werd' ich erst einmal einsam im Grabe sein' in the same song:

But too often Schumann is unable to sustain the force of such writing, so that the themes remain isolated and fragmentary. Most of the later songs show the influence of this declamatory technique, none more so than 'Stiller Vorwurf', which is pure recitative. The free verbal rhythms of opp. 89 and 90, and even those of the Düsseldorf songs right up to the Mary Stuart cycle, clearly descend from the fusion of symphonic and operatic methods which first showed itself in the Goethe songs, though there is no trace left of those methods in the idiom or mood of the music itself.

At the other end of the spectrum are Schumann's excursions into folk-song imitation, which, though less common than is often thought, are plentiful enough. The simpler children's songs in op. 79 are obviously of this type, and one is also inclined to place the Burns and Thomas Moore songs in this category. In the Kulmann songs, op. 104, Schumann clearly attempted a simple naivety akin to folk-song, though the actual result is very different. In none of these songs, even the very good Burns settings, is Schumann quite himself. He lacked the unselfconscious streak which enabled Schubert to re-create folk-song over and over again in the image of high art, and almost all his 'folk-song' essays are in some way contrived or artificial. 'Schlusslied des Narren' and 'Der Nussbaum' are both, in their contrasted ways, examples of music apparently in a folk style which, on examination, reveals the subtlety of expression and construction of a confirmed townsman.

It remains true that Schumann's greatest songs make their effect rather through harmony and texture than through melody. As a manipulator of harmony, Schumann is often underrated. It is true that the early 1840 songs do not share the harmonic versatility of the piano music; indeed the songs of opp. 24 and 25 tend to veer wildly between the very simple, even plain style of 'Morgens steh' ich auf' and the scarcely less simple but far from plain style of 'Die Lotosblume' or 'Widmung'. Even 'Der Nussbaum' and 'Jasminenstrauch', with their more elusive colouring, promise more harmonically than they achieve. But already there are pre-echoes of things to come (in the searching prelude to 'Ich wandelte unter den Bäumen' or the middle section of the same song, the dark chromatics of 'Aus den *Hebräischen Gesängen*', and less happily the obsequious chromatics of 'Was will die einsame Träne') though on the other hand Schumann never entirely lost his taste for the plain, rather hearty outdoor style of 'Freisinn', the pious chords of 'Zum Schluss', or the opulence of 'Widmung'.

As with most other aspects of Schumann's song-writing, it is in *Dichterliebe* that we find him using harmony with the greatest subtlety and versatility. Not that the harmonic idiom of this cycle is technically complicated. On the contrary, the technical elements of 'Im wunderschönen Monat Mai' or 'Wenn ich in deine Augen seh'' are far simpler than those of the *Wilhelm Meister* songs, whose language is thoroughly chromatic. Harmony in *Dichterliebe* is still basically diatonic, which means that a simple tune will be simply harmonized, except that at certain moments a sudden chromatic sideslip, or the faintest suggestion of doubt about the next chord (as at 'sprichst' in 'Wenn ich in deine Augen seh' ') will hint at some deeper feeling as yet unnoticed on the surface. It was this sparing but always apt use of chromaticism which Schumann found so hard to recapture in his later songs, partly because he never again found (or at any rate sympathized with) a poet so economical and pointed in expression as Heine. In *Frauenliebe und -leben* the harmony merely reverts to the simple opulence of 'Widmung' but without the freshness of that song. The songs of late 1840, on the other hand, already lean towards the heavier chromaticism of the 1849 style. 'Der Schatzgräber', for instance, though an imposing song in its way, is almost unrecognizable as the work of the composer of 'Hör' ich das Liedchen klingen'.

Schumann's later harmonic style was enriched from a number of different sources. The influence of Bach can be clearly heard in isolated songs, and more consistently in the last period, where expressive dissonance of a non-chromatic kind is a more or less regular feature. In 1849, however, Schumann was still partly under the spell of opera, and this accounts for the essentially dramatic nature of the harmony in the Goethe songs of that year. The chromaticism of op. 98 differs fundamentally from that of the 1840 songs in that, instead of being an expressive device within a more or less static harmonic framework, it has now become strongly functional and directional. 'Heiss' mich nicht reden' is a case in point. The song is in C minor, yet already after less than four bars there is a dramatic change to A flat on the word 'schweigen'— the key word of the poem. This is followed by an unstable series of progressions, through B flat minor and F minor, finally arriving back on a dominant minor ninth of the home key at the repeat of 'schweigen'. The middle section begins firmly in C major, but is soon veering towards the dominant and then the relative minor (though both cadences are interrupted) eventually modulating through A major to E major and thence via a series of diminished sevenths and German sixths into F, E flat minor, D flat and on to a crashing dominant seventh of C which itself fails to resolve until four bars later. If all this seems unduly elaborate, it at least shows how, in a short song of sixty-one bars, Schumann moves with almost excessive freedom through a whole series of improbable modulations. In a song of comparable length in *Dichterliebe*, 'Im Rhein, im heiligen Strome', there is hardly any real modulation at all. The song starts in E minor, where it stays for almost sixteen bars before slipping quietly into the relative major for a further eleven bars. Then follows the only unstable passage in the song, a chromatic interlude for piano starting on a thrillingly unexpected chord of E flat but drifting gradually back to A minor, the subdominant, for the last verse, which ends (characteristically) on a dominant chord. The postlude is solidly in E minor.

If modulation is an irregular feature of the 1840 songs, it is certainly not unknown. 'Ich wandelte unter den Bäumen' and 'Am leuchtenden Sommermorgen' (in B and B flat major respectively) both have verses in G major, though both otherwise stay close to the home key. 'Waldesgespräch' (in E major) has a verse in C, 'Widmung' (in A flat) a middle section in E, 'Die Lotosblume' (in F) one in A flat. But all are isolated switches to accommodate a single change of mood or scene, and in every case the new key, once established, is as stable in feeling as the old. It is in fact a possible criticism of the longer 1840 songs ('Schöne Wiege meiner Leiden' is one) that they are harmonically static. In the shorter songs too much movement would obviously destroy that sense of economy so vital to their effect, and this is indeed what happens in many of the 1850 lyrics, where chromaticism is so much the rule that the law of diminishing returns comes into play. If chromaticism equalled expressiveness, 'Kommen und Scheiden' would be one of Schumann's most moving songs. In fact it is one of his least effective.

Most of the song collections are arranged in key sequence, and it is generally within some such plan that Schumann will end a song in a key other than its own home tonic. Almost always the device has an air of contrivance. We do not, for instance, feel any special unity within the Lenau set op. 90, despite the elaborate manipulation of keys so that each song follows on from the last. In op. 35 there is no clear internal reason why 'Stirb, Lieb' und Freud'!' should end on the dominant of the next song, 'Wanderlust'. Significantly neither of the two best collections, *Dichterliebe* and the Eichendorff *Liederkreis*, uses the device, though they of all Schumann's cycles would have the most justification for doing so. But their unity, already discussed in Chapter III, is at a deeper psychological level, and needs no artificial reinforcement.

Perhaps the most consistently weak component of Schumann's songs—the area to which failure can most often be traced—is rhythm. As a habitual composer for a solo instrument, he found word-setting a formidable challenge to his independence and love of free-ranging fantasy, and many of his songs, especially those of 1840, are seriously restricted by verbal metre. The ballads provide the most obvious examples, as well as the most disastrous, perhaps because—in, for instance, a song like 'Blondels Lied'—the musical surrender is so complete. Even in a far more specifically 'musical' ballad-setting like 'Belsatzar', the music's growth is shackled by a verbal or poetic phrase-structure, which insists on a regular two-bar grouping with the musical syllables crammed more or less regularly in between. But there was more to this than a simple acquiescence in a poetic metre, for Schumann was perfectly capable of boxing an irregular poem into a neat, square carton, as he does with Goethe's 'Freisinn'—merely pretending that the box is at least oblong by anticipating each vocal phrase in the accompaniment. Here it is the instrument (i.e., the voice) rather than the words which holds his fantasy in check.

That Schumann was aware of this failing is clear from the sometimes artificial means by which he tried to combat it. The interpolated piano phrase comes often to his rescue, if seldom so transparently as in 'Freisinn', and there are other instances where the device succeeds by a species of double-bluff in which the interlude, though itself predictable, fails to behave in the expected way. In 'Weit, weit', for instance, Schumann avoids the obvious trap of a single extra bar in the song's six–eight time, whose effect would be that of a till-ready, and instead draws the bar out by an extra compound beat, surprising the ear into accepting it as a positive contribution to the music. In 'Er, der Herrlichste von allen' he three times interrupts the voice with imitative entries of the main theme in the piano, which conceal the rather conventional modulatory function of these bars while at the same time lending asymmetry to the rhythm by anticipating the listener's expectation of where this theme will restart. The most brilliant example of all comes, predictably, in one of the *Dichterliebe* songs, 'Am leuchtenden Sommermorgen'. The tune of this song is essentially simple (though not folklike) but Schumann complicates it with an added bar of accompaniment before each couplet, always using the same German sixth chord sequence as in the song's introduction. Before the final couplet, however, there is no interpolation, so that the asymmetry itself becomes asymmetrical; the flowers cut in, as it were, on the poet's thoughts with the new idea of forgiveness, on which the long postlude will muse.

Another favourite device is the repetition of words or lines. We have seen that Schumann often used repetition to spin out a poem which was too short for his musical needs ('Er ist's', 'Nur wer die Sehnsucht kennt', 'Stille Tränen'). But single words could also be repeated in order to break the verbal, and thereby the rhythmic, symmetry. 'Morgens steh' ich auf', with its trance-like repetitions of 'auch heut' ', 'lieg' ich' and 'träumend', is a neat and effective example. Still more attractive is the Thomas Moore song, 'Leis' rudern hier', where the repeated 'leis'' and 'sacht' have a hypnotic beauty which amply compensates for the scrappy declamation elsewhere in this piece. The device is sparingly used in *Dichterliebe*, and always with nicely calculated effect. The repeats in 'Ich grolle nicht', for instance, are intended—and work—ironically; in 'Das ist ein Flöten und Geigen', line-repeats are used to stretch the vocal phrases unequally over the more or less regular frame provided by the accompaniment. Perhaps the most original example of all is 'Allnächtlich im Traume', where Schumann completely re-forms Heine's scansion, with the help of a single repetition and an irregular barring, to produce a sense of unease and restless introspection. One can think of few better instances in music of the art that conceals art.

It is not to be argued, of course, that Schumann's songs as a whole are rhythmically inept, only that when inspiration is at a low ebb it is most frequently in the rhythm that one feels a sense of squareness or routine. A common danger signal is repeated quaver chords in the piano, which seem to have stood for solidity and security in Schumann's mind (curiously enough, many of the admired examples of such figuration—'Die Lotosblume', 'Widmung', 'Mondnacht', 'Du bist wie eine Blume', though not 'Ich grolle nicht'—are written in crotchet or semiquaver notation). On the other hand, Schumann had a genius for making a square vocal metre sound anything but plain by the use of subtly varied rhythmic dispositions in the piano part. 'Ich wandelte unter den Bäumen' is a good example of a song whose interest depends to a large extent on minute cross-rhythms, syncopations, anticipations of the downbeat, and so on. In later life, when experience of dramatic writing had more or less emancipated his feeling for vocal rhythm, Schumann tended to overdo inflections of this kind. 'Abendlied' and 'Der Gärtner' are both inspired works marred by pernickety rhythmic detail, and in songs like 'Aufträge' or 'Singet nicht in Trauertönen' one yearns for the Schumann of 'Widmung', who knew how much of a poet's metric scheme to retain and how much to alter for the subtlest musical effect.

When all this is said, it remains true that many of Schumann's best songs adhere closely to the broad metre of their verse, varying it only in internal detail. 'Am leuchtenden Sommermorgen' is exceptional among the 'flower' songs of *Dichterliebe* in going beyond the phrase structure of its poem, while 'Im wunderschönen Monat Mai', 'Die Rose, die Lilie', 'Ich will meine Seele tauchen', 'Und wüssten's die Blumen' and 'Hör' ich das Liedchen klingen' all respect Heine's scansion, relying on tiny alterations (like the triplet on 'wunderbar' at the end of 'Ich will meine Seele tauchen') and elusive piano figuration and harmony to provide psychological insight. Strictly analysed, these songs are as square in cut as any of the ballads or march-songs. But their simplicity, instead of being underlined by the accompaniment, harmony and internal rhythms, is merely one projection of a complex thought—like the flat surface of a deep pool. The beauty is all the greater for the apparent blandness of what first presents itself to the ear.

One other method which Schumann used to conceal dullness of rhythm was the gradual *accelerando* or, less often, *decelerando*. The device is significantly absent from *Dichterliebe*, but turns up with fair regularity in most other phases of the songs, and is perhaps the nearest thing in them to a mannerism. In a few cases ('Intermezzo', 'Die Lotosblume', perhaps 'Abends am Strand') one feels that the changing tempo properly reflects increasing tension in the music; at other times it shows the composer's awareness of tensions in the poem which are not truly reflected in the music ('Belsatzar' is a clear instance of this; in 'Frühlingsfahrt' a *decelerando* is used for the opposite purpose). At its worst the trick merely alerts the listener to the music's failure to sustain its thought from beginning to end. In 'Requiem' and 'Sängers Trost' the marking *nach und nach belebter/bewegter* states frankly that the composer has had enough of this material and would like to get to the end of the poem as quickly as possible. The added tension inevitably seems spurious.

As this procedure suggests, Schumann was neither at his best nor at his happiest in the larger-scale type of song. He never mastered, as Schubert had, the art of sustained through-composition in lyric style, and most of his attempts, from 'Belsatzar' to 'Einsamkeit', more or less outstay their welcome. In fact the greater number of Schumann's more extended songs date from 1849-50, when his musical speech had become more expansive as a result of experience in symphony and opera. However, the best examples, 'Ich wandelte unter den Bäumen', 'Der Nussbaum', 'Aus den *Hebräischen Gesängen*', 'Mondnacht' and 'Zwielicht' are all early, and of these all but two are cast in forms of a strophic or episodic character, rather than being through-composed in the manner of most of the songs in Schubert's *Winterreise* or Schumann's own later *Wilhelm Meister* settings. The two exceptions, 'Der Nussbaum' and 'Mondnacht', rank among that considerable number of songs where Schumann created an entirely original form out of the verse and the musical material it inspired. In both songs the material itself is used with great economy, a short melodic phrase recurring hypnotically over and over (of the six vocal phrases in 'Mondnacht', five are identical, apart from a slight variation at the end of the last).

In his song forms Schumann was essentially an experimenter. He made little use of strophic form in the classic or folk sense, where the music is written out once only, with the text for each verse printed underneath. Yet a large number of his songs—perhaps one in five—are in all essentials strophic, but with varied accompaniments, changes in the structure of the vocal line, changes from major to minor, and so on. Where strophic form seems to be the natural way of expressing a poem, Schumann makes no attempt to avoid it, but tries to weld the form into a continuous unit so that the listener is unconscious of the repetitions. Inevitably he sometimes misjudges, as Schubert often did, the aptness of his music to every verse of the poem, yet even in such cases the sense of continuity, and the small adjustments permitted by a written-out format, may well disguise all but the worst incongruities, where in Schubert (a famous example is 'Die liebe Farbe') they are apparent, for better or worse, to all.

With episodic forms Schumann was not always so successful, mainly because designs of this kind (ternary form is the simplest, rondo form the most elaborate) are usually preconceived and seldom suit a poem exactly. In many of his songs of this kind, as we noted earlier, Schumann had to repeat the poem's first verse in order to round the music off with the necessary return of the main theme—often, as in 'Meine Rose', with disastrous consequences for the sense of the words, though occasionally, as in the less contrasted 'Intermezzo' or 'Widmung', with good effect. Schumann seems to have taken a less experimental view of ternary than of strophic form, a fact which underlines the essentially musical, rather than poetic, character of this type of structure. However, in his later songs, especially those of 1850, ternary form often appears with a heavily varied reprise, as in 'Himmel und Erde', where only the key and piano figuration tell us that an ABA design is intended. Such writing strongly suggests piano music (but not particularly Schumann's; one feels the influence of Chopin's nocturnes).

Few of Schumann's greatest songs are cast in episodic forms, and though his experiments in strophic design are generally more interesting and successful, it was as a miniaturist that he attained greatest mastery. The term 'miniature' needs definition. In one sense, of course, ninety-five per cent of Schumann's songs are miniatures. But in trying to distinguish work that is essentially miniaturistic from that which is merely small-scale, we could say that a true miniature is a lowest common denominator of musical form—a kind of irreducible (if not necessarily unanalysable) prime number. Such a definition would be satisfied by most of the songs in *Dichterliebe*, and by a handful of other songs from 1840, but by few composed after that year. Like most definitions, this one cannot be pressed too far. Rigidly applied it would deny that 'Setze mir nicht' or 'Im wunderschönen Monat Mai' are miniatures, which is absurd. But it does point an ideal to which Schumann perhaps came closer than any other song-writer—an ideal of conciseness and economy which, by something more cogent than coincidence, we find approached in almost all his most telling songs.

The short setting in one verse with piano introduction and/or postlude is the characteristic Schumann song-form, and significantly the most perfect examples are to poems of Heine. The typical Heine lyric is terse, epigrammatic, highly intense, and above all single-minded (in the sense that it broaches only one central idea). Heine's language is simple and direct, but his meaning tends to be ambivalent, and for a composer this is the vital quality since it leaves open a whole area of interpretation which it is music's special function to explore. In Schumann the duality is expressed by a tune and its accompaniment. In 'Ich will meine Seele tauchen', to take one of the very best examples, the tune itself, like the poet's language, is of extreme simplicity and is confined, like that of 'Aus meinen Tränen spriessen', to six notes of the home key (in this case B minor). The imagery of the poem, however, is by no means simple: 'I would plunge my soul into the lily's chalice, so that, in vibrating, the lily might breathe a song from my beloved, trembling like the kiss she once gave me in a wonderful sweet hour!' The associations are sexual, but veiled rather than explicit, and Schumann perfectly catches the sense of quivering excitement in the demisemiquavers of the piano's left hand. At the same time there is an indefinable sense of loss, expressed mainly by the final line of the poem, and, in the song, by a forlorn countersubject in the piano's right hand. And just as Heine leaves us with a sense of something beautiful but no longer within reach, so Schumann runs his countersubject into a postlude where the sense of loss wells up to dominate the memory of what is lost, so that an image of beauty becomes an image of pain and remorse:

Such a song does not occur in the work of any other composer, not even that of Wolf, who shared (as the *Italian Songbook* demonstrates) Schumann's flair for concise utterance but not his gift—which was also Heine's—for expressing deep feeling in the simplest language. Wolf almost certainly recognized this superiority in his predecessor. His Heine settings include only two—and those very early—of poems set by Schumann, and his more mature Eichendorff songs none at all, a sure sign of his profound respect for the existing versions. Wolf's opinion of Schumann's songs was in fact higher than that held by most present-day singers. According to Frank Walker, he told Paul Müller that two-thirds of Schumann's lieder had lasting musical value—that is, some 160. Perhaps a third of that number (less than a quarter of the total) are familiar to modern audiences. The reason for this neglect is clear enough. The Heine, Eichendorff and Chamisso cycles are popular—quite apart from their musical quality—

because they lend themselves to integral performance by one singer. Outside these collections, however, many of the best songs are rather short, whereas most recitalists like to feel that in learning new material they are filling substantial holes in their repertoires. So it is that Schumann groups in mixed recitals tend to be made up of agreeable but second-rate music (one such group, which figured in a London recital programme during 1970, consisted of 'Der arme Peter', 'Die Blume der Ergebung', 'Lied der Suleika', 'Er ist's', and 'Singet nicht in Trauertonen').

But Wolf's evaluation is not exaggerated, provided it is musical interest, rather than artistic perfection, which is taken as the criterion for what is worth performing. Schumann's songs are certainly very uneven in quality, and his poorest efforts are probably worse than those of any of the great songwriters, not excluding Schubert. But looking between the obvious masterpieces and the undeniable failures, there remains a substantial area of characteristic, fascinating and often inspired music which holds out real rewards to the singer and listener who are prepared to explore it. One could cite op. 25 (*Myrten*), the Kerner songs op. 35, the Andersen songs op. 40, the Goethe songs op. 98a, and the miscellaneous op. 107, as collections whose musical quality might surprise those who imagine that Schumann wrote few songs of value outside the well-known cycles. They do not, of course, contain much to set beside the finest things in *Dichterliebe*, all in all probably Schumann's greatest work. But it is a poor musical culture that has no time for the characteristic secondary works of those composers whom, on account of their masterpieces, it considers to be geniuses.

Index

Abendlied, 101–2, 119
Abends am Strand, 23, 65
Abschied vom Walde, 89
Abschied von der Welt, 100
Abschied von Frankreich, 100, 109
Allnächtlich im Traume, 49, 118
Alte Laute, 69
Am leuchtenden Sommermorgen, 48–9, 50, 107, 111, 112, 116, 118, 119
An Anna (I), 5*n*, 6
An Anna (II), 6
An den Mond, 87
An den Sonnenschein, 64
An die Königin Elisabeth, 99–100
An die Türen will ich schleichen, 86
Anfangs wollt' ich, 26
An meinem Herzen, 55
Auf das Trinkglas eines verstorbenen Freundes, 65, 70, 71–2, 109
Auf dem Rhein, 109
Auf einer Burg, 38, 39, 57
Aufträge, 89–90, 109
Aus alten Märchen winkt es, 49–50
Aus den *Hebräischen Gesängen*, 30, 35, 109, 114, 120
Aus den *Östlichen Rosen*, 28
Aus meinen Tränen spriessen, 42, 43, 44, 122
Ballade des Harfners, 86
Belsatzar, 21, 23, 57, 58, 86, 105, 117, 120
Berg und Burgen, 26–7, 105, 112
Blondels Lied, 58, 66, 109, 117
Da liegt der Feinde, 103
Das ist ein Flöten und Geigen, 22, 43, 47, 62, 78, 110, 118
Das verlassene Mägdelein, 78, 105, 108, 109

Dein Angesicht, 51
Dem Helden, 87
Dem roten Röslein, 17, 19, 112
Den grünen Zeigern, 103
Der arme Peter, 18, 21, 22–3, 47, 62, 124
Der Bräutigam und die Birke, 100
Der Contrabandiste, 79, 105
Der Einsiedler, 40, 92, 109
Der frohe Wandersmann, 35
Der Gärtner, 100, 101, 111, 119
Der Handschuh, 105
Der Hidalgo, 59–60, 100
Der Himmel hat eine Träne geweint, 72–3, 104
Der Husar, trara!, 103
Der Knabe mit dem Wunderhorn, 59, 69
Der leidige Frieden, 102
Der Nussbaum, 27–8, 33, 37, 89, 105, 114, 120
Der Page, 59
Der Sandmann, 83, 109
Der Schatzgräber, 40*n*, 65, 105, 115
Der schwere Abend, 93, 94
Der Soldat, 60, 61–2, 63, 77
Der Spielmann, 60, 62–3
Des Buben Schützenlied, 82
Des Sennen Abschied, 82
DICHTERLIEBE (Heine), *op. 48*, 5, 10, 13, 16, 26, 28, 30 & *n*, 32, 40, **41–52**, 53, 55, 56, 70, 73, 78, 95, 98, 103, 105–6, 107, 108, 110–11, 112, 114–15, 117, 118, 119, 122, 124
Dichters Genesung, 64
Die alten, bösen Lieder, 41, 48, 50, 94, 111
Die beiden Grenadiere, 21–2, 57, 62
Die Blume der Ergebung, 90, 109, 113, 124

© Cassell & Co., Ltd, 1971

Die feindlichen Brüder, 21–2
Die Fensterscheibe, 98
Die Hochländer-Witwe, 18, 19
Die Hütte, 100
Die Kartenlegerin, 58–9, 63, 98, 100, 105
Die Lotosblume, 23, 24, 27, 34, 35, 40, 68, 105, 114, 116, 119, 120
Die Löwenbraut, 25, 57–8
Die Meerfee, 90
Die Nonne, 66–7, 106, 108
Die Rose, die Lilie, 44, 45, 119
Die rote Hanne, 57–8, 70, 72
Die Sennin, 92, 93
Die Soldatenbraut, 77–8
Die Spinnerin, 99
Die Stille, 37, 44
Die Tochter Jephta's, 87
Die wandelnde Glocke, 82, 108
DREI GEDICHTE (Geibel), *op. 30*, 51, 57, **59–60**
DREI GEDICHTE (Pfarrius), *op. 119*, **100**
DREI GESÄNGE (Chamisso), *op. 31*, 27, **57–9**
DREI GESÄNGE (Byron), *op. 95*, 30, 78, **86–7**
Du bist wie eine Blume, 23–4, 26, 29, 42, 109, 112, 119
Du Ring an meinem Finger, 54, 112
Ein Gedanke, 29–30
Ein Jüngling liebt ein Mädchen, 41, 48
Einsamkeit, 92, 93, 110, 120
Er, der Herrlichste von allen, 53–4, 55, 74, 81, 112, 117
Er ist's, 82, 105, 106, 124
Erste Begegnung, 79
Erstes Grün, 70, 111
Es leuchtet meine Liebe, 51, 108
Es stürmet am Abendhimmel, 88, 109
Es treibt mich hin, 25, 26, 110
Flügel! Flügel!, 73
Flutenreicher Ebro, 79
Frage, 69
FRAUENLIEBE UND -LEBEN (Chamisso), *op. 42*, 27, 29, 50, 51, **52–6**, 57, 107, 109, 111, 115

Freisinn, 16, 35, 65, 69, 100, 114, 117
Frühlingsfahrt, 40*n*, 65, 120
Frühlingsgruss, 102
Frühlingslied, 91
Frühlingslust, 90, 109
Frühlingsnacht, 35, 39–40, 94, 108
FÜNF LIEDER, *op. 40*, 51, 57, **60–3**, 65, 124
FÜNF LIEDER UND GESANGE, *op. 127*, 14, 51
Gebet, 99, 100
GEDICHTE AUS LIEBESFRÜHLING (Rückert), *op. 37*, 27, **72–4**
GEDICHTE DER KÖNIGIN MARIA STUART, *op. 135*, 25, 27, **99–100**, 113
Geisternähe, 90
Gesanges Erwachen, 5*n*
Geständnis, 79
Gesungen, 88, 89, 109
Hauptmanns Weib, 18
Heimliches Verschwinden, 89
Heiss mich nicht reden, 85, 109, 111, 115
Helft mir, ihr Schwestern, 53, 55–6
Herbstlied, 88, 109
Herzeleid, 96, 97, 98, 100
Himmel und Erde, 89, 97, 109, 121
Hirtenknabe, 6
Hoch, hoch sind die Berge, 80, 108
Hochländers Abschied, 17–18
Hochländisches Wiegenlied, 18, 19, 108
Hör ich das Liedchen klingen, 47–8, 70, 89, 106, 115, 119
Husarenabzug, 89, 102
Ich grolle nicht, 46, 109, 110, 119
Ich hab' im Traum geweinet, 49, 93
Ich hab' in mich gesogen, 73–4
Ich kann's nicht fassen, 54
Ich wandelte unter den Bäumen, 27, 29, 33, 40, 48, 69, 108, 112, 114, 116, 119, 120
Ich wand're nicht, 74
Ich will meine Seele tauchen, 45–6, 108, 119, 122

INDEX

Ihre Stimme, 89, 97, 112
Im Herbste, 6
Im Rhein, im heiligen Strome, 46, 116
Im Wald, 98–9, 108
Im Walde, 39
Im Westen, 20, 80
Im wunderschönen Monat Mai, 42, 44, 53, 61, 90, 110, 112, 114, 119, 122
In der Fremde (I), 35, 36
In der Fremde (II), 38–9
In der Nacht, 79
Ins Freie, 89, 109
Intermezzo, 35, 36, 51, 79, 106, 112, 120, 121
Jasminenstrauch, 19, 28, 34, 61, 89, 106, 114
Jemand, 19–20
Jung Volkers Lied, 100–1, 106
Käuzlein, 82
Kennst du das Land?, 82, 83, 84, 85, 109
Kommen und Scheiden, 92, 93, 116
Kurzes Erwachen, 5n
Lehn' deine Wang', 51
Leis' rudern hier, 31, 107, 118
Liebesbotschaft, 64
Liebesgram, 79
Liebeslied, 89, 112
Lieb' Liebchen, 24, 25, 47, 110, 112
Liebste, was kann denn uns scheiden, 73
Liebster, deine Worte stehlen, 81
Lieder der Braut, 28–9, 110
Lied der Suleika, 16, 19, 26, 69, 106, 112, 124
Lied eines Schmiedes, 93, 107
LIEDER UND GESÄNGE, *op. 27*, 19
LIEDER UND GESÄNGE, *op. 51*, 29, 57
LIEDER UND GESÄNGE, *op. 77*, 35
LIEDER UND GESÄNGE, *op. 96*, 88, 89
LIEDER UND GESÄNGE AUS 'WILHELM MEISTER' (Goethe), *op. 98*, 15, 30, 78, **82–6**, 95, 104, 109, 113, 114, 115, 120, 124
LIEDERALBUM FÜR DIE JUGEND, *op. 79*, 64, 77, 78, **81–3**, 84, 91, 96, 113
LIEDERKREIS (Heine), *op. 24*, 13, 23, **24–7**, 34, 35, 53, 108, 111–12, 114, 123–4
LIEDERKREIS (Eichendorff), *op. 39* 13, 15, 24, 27, 30n, **32–40**, 43, 56, 59, 108, 123–4
Lied Lynceus des Türmers, 82
Loreley, 28n
Lust der Sturmnacht, 67–8
Mädchen-Schwermut, 66, 74, 78
Marienwürmchen, 83
Märzveilchen, 60–1, 111
Mein altes Ross, 92
Meine Rose, 93, 103, 106, 121
Meine Töne still und heiter, 80, 81
Mein Garten, 91
Mein Herz ist schwer, 30
Mein schöner Stern, 81
Mein Wagen rollet langsam, 51, 111
Melancholie, 79
MINNESPIEL AUS LIEBESFRÜHLING (Rückert), *op. 101*, 78, **80–1**
Mit Myrten und Rosen, 26, 41, 107
Mondnacht, 37–8, 119, 120
Morgens steh' ich auf und frage, 24, 25, 96, 112, 113, 118
Muttertraum, 30, 39, 60, 61, 62, 86, 93, 105, 109
MYRTEN, *op. 25*, 13, **15–20**, 23–4, 25, 26, **27–9**, 30–1, 34, 36, 53, 75, 98, 108, 114, 124
Nach der Geburt ihres Sohnes, 99
Nachtlied, 15–16, 91–2, 95, 102, 109, 111
Nichts Schöneres, 63–4, 74
Niemand, 18, 108
Nun hast du mir den ersten Schmerz getan, 18, 55
Nur ein lächelnder Blick, 66, 72, 104
Nur wer die Sehnsucht kennt, 85, 118
O Freund, mein Schirm, mein Schutz, 81, 83, 109–10
O ihr Herren, 73–4
O Sonn', o Meer, o Rose, 73

O wie lieblich ist das Mädchen, 80
Rätsel, 30–1, 105
Requiem, 92, 94, 109, 120
Resignation, 90, 113
ROMANZEN UND BALLADEN, op. *45*, 40 & *n*, 65
ROMANZEN UND BALLADEN, op. *49*, 21–2
Röselein, Röselein, 88–9, 109
Rose, Meer und Sonne, 73
Sag' an, o lieber Vogel mein, 30
Sängers Trost, 72, 120
Schlusslied des Narren, 10, 14–15, 98, 105, 114
Schmetterling, 82
Schneeglöckchen (anon.), 90, 91
Schneeglöckchen (Rückert), 82
Schöne Fremde, 35, 37, 38, 40, 68, 108
Schöne Wiege meiner Leiden, 26, 34–5, 106, 110, 116
SECHS GEDICHTE (Renick), op. *36*, 51, **63–4**
SECHS GEDICHTE UND 'REQUIEM' (Lenau), op. *90*, 30*n*, **92–4**, 95, 113, 116
SECHS GESÄNGE (v.d. Neun), op. *89*, **88–9**, 93, 104, 113
Sehnsucht (Ebert), 5
Sehnsucht (Geibel), 60, 109
Sehnsucht nach der Waldgegend, 70, 72
Seit ich ihn gesehen, 53, 108
Setze mir nicht, 17, 98, 105, 122
SIEBEN LIEDER (Kuhlmann), op. *104*, 96, 104, 114
Singet nicht in Trauertönen, 83, 85, 98, 109, 119, 124
Sitz' ich allein, 16, 17
So lasst mich scheinen, 85, 107
Soldatenleid, 77
Sonntag, 83
Sonntags am Rhein, 63, 106
SPANISCHE LIEBESLIEDER, op. *138*, 78, **79–80**
SPANISCHES LIEDERSPIEL, op. *74*, **78–9**

Ständchen, 64
Stille Liebe, 69, 70
Stiller Vorwurf, 90, 113
Stille Tränen, 68–9, 106, 111, 118
Stirb, Lieb' und Freud'!, 67*n*, 70–1, 116
Süsser Freund, 55
Talismane, 16
Tief im Herzen, 79
Tragödie, 21, 40, 74, 78
Trost im Gesang, 72
Und wüssten's die Blumen, 46–7, 106, 110, 119
Verratene Liebe, 57*n*, 60, 63
VIER GESÄNGE, op. *142*, 51
VIER HUSARENLIEDER (Lenau), op. *117*, 89, 90, **102–3**
Volksliedchen, 29
Vom Schlaraffenland, 31
Waldesgespräch, 35, 36–7, 107, 116
Wanderlust, 67*n*, 69, 77, 116
Wanderung, 69–70
Warnung, 110
Warte, wilder Schiffsmann, 24, 26
Was soll ich sagen, 27, 57, 107
Was will die einsame Träne, 23, 114
Wehmut, 39, 40, 64, 106, 108
Weh, wie zornig, 79
Wenn durch die Piazetta, 31
Wenn ich in deine Augen seh', 20–1, 40, 45, 105, 107, 110, 114, 115
Wer machte dich so krank, 67, 69
Wer nie sein Brod mit Tränen ass, 86
Wer sich der Einsamkeit ergibt, 85–6, 106, 113
Widmung, 15, 29, 53, 55, 72, 73, 106, 112, 114, 115, 116, 119, 121
Zigeunerliedchen, 83
Zum Schluss, 15, 28, 73, 114
Zwielicht, 30, 35, 39, 61, 93, 109, 120
ZWÖLF GEDICHTE (Kerner), op. *35*, 66, **67–72**, 111, 116, 124